Real Math

ENGLISH LEARNER SUPPORT GUIDE

Grade 4

Stephen S. Willoughby

•

Carl Bereiter

•

Peter Hilton

•

Joseph H. Rubinstein

•

Joan Moss

•

Jean J. Pedersen

•

Elizabeth Jimenez

Columbus, OH

The **McGraw·Hill** Companies

SRAonline.com

 **SRA**

Send all inquiries to:
SRA/McGraw-Hill
8787 Orion Place
Columbus, OH 43240-4027

ISBN 0-07-604354-1

1 2 3 4 5 6 7 8 9 BCH 12 11 10 09 08 07 06

English Learner Support Guide Lessons

Table of Contents

English Learner Support Guide Lessons

Using Real Math

Real Math is a comprehensive, elementary-grade mathematics program designed to
- teach **basic skills** with **understanding** so they can be used with fluency to solve real problems.
- build mathematical thinking to **reason** about, understand, and **apply** mathematics in order to identify, solve, and communicate about real problems.
- **engage** students in mathematics so they enjoy math and see it as understandable and useful.

Beginning in the earliest grade levels, *Real Math* develops the content strands of mathematics so children learn how the strands are integrated, how to develop number sense, and how to learn the language of mathematics.

Arithmetic, including counting, addition, subtraction, multiplication, division

Algebra, including patterns, functions, and variables

Geometry

Measurement

Data Collection and Organization, including graphs and charts

Probability and Statistics

Rational Numbers, including fractions, decimals, and percentages

Number Sense and Place Value

Mathematical Proficiency

Real Math builds mathematical proficiency in every lesson.

Mathematical proficiency has five strands. These strands are not independent; they represent different aspects of a complex whole. They are interwoven and interdependent in the development of proficiency in mathematics.

1 Understanding (Conceptual Understanding): comprehending mathematical concepts, operations, and relations—knowing what mathematical symbols, diagrams, and procedures mean

2 Computing (Procedural Fluency): carrying out mathematical procedures, such as adding, subtracting, multiplying, and dividing numbers flexibly, accurately, efficiently, and appropriately

3 Applying (Strategic Competence): being able to formulate problems mathematically and to devise strategies for solving them using concepts and procedures appropriately

4 Reasoning (Adaptive Reasoning): using logic to explain and justify a solution to a problem, or to extend from something known to something not yet known

5 Engaging (Productive Disposition): seeing mathematics as sensible, useful, and doable—*if* you work at it—and being willing to do the work

From Kilpatrick, J.; Swafford, J.; and Findell, B. eds. *Adding It Up: Helping Children Learn Mathematics.* Washington, D.C.: National Research Council/ National Academy Press, 2001, pp. 115–133.

Real Math and Math Proficiency

The goals of *Real Math* are to develop the five interwoven proficiencies. In every lesson, activities are designed to address understanding, computing, reasoning, applying, and engaging in an integrated fashion.

Using the *English Learner Support Guide*

The *English Learner Support Guide* provides teachers with valuable tools to meet the needs of English learners. Often English learners understand the mathematics in a lesson, but cannot communicate that understanding in English.

For each *Real Math* lesson, the *English Learner Support Guide* includes a lesson plan for teachers, teacher's aides, or parent volunteers to follow to Preview and Review the lesson for students learning English. Spanish is included for teacher convenience, although the same concepts can be translated to other languages.

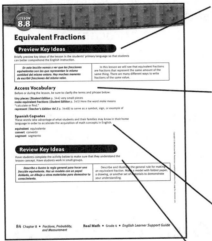

English Learner Support Guide

Preview Key Ideas is designed to help teachers provide the key ideas of the lesson in the students' primary language. If students understand the key ideas before the lesson begins, they can often follow along more coherently.

Access Vocabulary provides an overview of common phrases, idioms, and colloquialisms that will come up in the lesson that may not be familiar to English learners. Teachers who are aware of these terms and phrases can help English learners better understand the lesson concepts at the same time they develop vocabulary.

Spanish Cognates, words or root words that are the same or similar in English, help to take advantage of what students and their families may already know about mathematics.

Review Key Ideas offers a chance for English learners to summarize their understanding in their primary language and for teachers to assess that understanding.

When to Use *English Learner Support Guide* Activities

The *English Learner Support Guide* activities are intended to be used at the following times:

Before the Lesson

Preview Key Ideas A routine can be established with English learners to gather together five minutes before math with the teacher, a teacher's aide, or a parent volunteer to preview the key ideas.

During the Lesson

Teachers can address the **Access Vocabulary** and **Spanish Cognates** during the lesson by explaining and defining vocabulary and pointing out similarities between English and Spanish. This type of vocabulary instruction has been proven to be highly effective.

After the Lesson

Review Key Ideas A routine can be established with English learners to gather after the lesson with the teacher, a teacher's aide, or a parent volunteer to review key ideas and assess student understanding of lesson concepts.

Assessing *English Learner* Activities

The Preview and Review of Key Ideas with English learners provides an excellent opportunity to informally assess these students' understanding of mathematics and the English language.

Differentiating Instruction

During these short sessions, teachers can determine whether students need math enrichment, practice, reteaching, or intervention. The *Enrichment, Practice, Reteach,* and *Intervention* materials might be appropriate for homework.

Teachers can also determine how much more or less language support students need and adjust their instruction accordingly.

English Learners

When students do not speak the language of the school, they face some enormous challenges. They must learn the new language, keep up with the other students in the academic arena, and adjust to a new set of expectations and cultural routines that may not be clear to the student or the family. When the school does not speak the language of the student, the school community faces some demanding challenges as well. They must find ways to communicate with the student and the family, starting with the enrollment process and continuing instructionally throughout the year. Teachers must provide comprehensible academic input by adjusting their instructional techniques, and the school community needs to be as clear and explicit as possible about its expectations for behavior, participation, and learning, while keeping in mind that the student may be accustomed to a very different system of educational norms.

The most powerful instruction for English learners is that which is designed on a blueprint of inclusion. This allows English learners to interact with proficient speakers of English who serve as language models and provide authentic practice for speaking and listening.

Real Math and English Learners

Real Math is carefully designed to include English learners by utilizing the expert sheltered techniques and strategies found in research and best practices. Its powerful design incorporates many widely used techniques that enhance English language acquisition while making new math concepts comprehensible. By designing these techniques into the very fabric of the mathematics program, *Real Math* makes it easy for teachers to address the needs of all students without having to do a lot of ancillary preparation.

Levels of English Proficiency

English learners enter schools at different grade levels and bring varying levels of English proficiency and academic preparation attained in their primary language. Some students have high levels of academic preparation that allow them to focus more on learning the terminology associated with the math skills they already know. These students have a great advantage as they already understand that mathematics has its own terminology and have a grasp of the basic skills and concepts needed to participate in advancing their math skills.

Other students may have had little schooling or interrupted school experiences, which means that they need to catch up to their grade-level peers academically, and they must begin the task of English acquisition at the same time. Many schools use some form of primary language instruction or support to accelerate students' skill base while learning English. This approach contains the added advantage of being able to rely on the student's family as a source of support and inclusion.

Currently every state is required to develop English Language Development standards and to identify an English proficiency test that is used throughout the state to identify English learners, to evaluate English Language progress annually, and to help determine when students are fully proficient and can be redesignated as Fluent English Proficient. Most state tests use a proficiency scale of four or five levels that may be labeled in various terms. Knowing the continuum of English Language Development may be very helpful in determining where students are and how to move them to the next level of English proficiency. The best place to begin is with the data from your English proficiency test to determine the students' English strengths and areas for further development.

When students are new to English, they go through predictable stages of English Language acquisition. The chart on the next page is a description of what we might observe in English learners as they cross the language proficiency continuum, some instructional strategies that are widely used to enhance comprehension, a reflection on some typical language-development patterns for a young child learning the first language, and a comparison of second-language learners' predicted rate of acquisition of English as a second language.

Levels of Proficiency Continuum

	Early Production	Emergent	Intermediate	High Intermediate/ Transitional
Characteristic Speaker Behaviors	• Trying to comprehend messages • Getting used to sounds, e.g., rhythms and intonations	• Single word phrases, e.g., *yes, no* • Short, fixed phrases • Routine expressions	• Slowly expanding vocabulary and grammar • Produces longer phrases • Acquiring communicative competence	• Apparently fluent • Completes sentences • More extensive vocabulary • Correctness level improves
Instructional Strategies	Total Physical Response • Questions that elicit *yes* or *no* answers • Gestures such as pointing, picking up, demonstrating • Activities that allow student participation • Comprehensible input	Total Physical Response • Questions that ask for: *Either/or* sentence completion Elicit lists • Teach use of cognates • Explain idioms and cultural expressions • Comprehensible input	Questions that ask for: Comparing Describing Sequencing • Teach use of cognates • Explain idioms and cultural expressions • Comprehensible input	Questions that require critical-thinking skills • Language experience approach to reading • Narration • Explain idioms, sayings, and expressions, as well as cultural assumptions
Time Line for: Acquisition of L1	Birth to one year	9 months–2 years	2–5 years	5 years and older
Time Line for: Acquisition of L2	Children: 3–6 months Adults: 10 hours	6 months–1 year	2–3 years	Ongoing

Academic Language Acquisition

English learners often sound fluent in conversation, which leads teachers to believe that they are completely proficient in English in all settings. Social conversation is often concrete, discussing events and subjects shared by those in conversation. However, academic language, the language that allows us to discuss abstract concepts, employs sophisticated grammatical constructions. These may include passive voice, literary devices such as metaphor, and even humor. These constructions are complex yet extremely important for the school success of all students, including English learners.

Mathematics, like all content-area subjects, has a special language that helps us learn key concepts and discuss them with others. This academic language includes the unique terminology of mathematics, as well as the signs and symbols that are used to convey common understandings. The academic language of mathematics is not usually encountered in social settings, such as home, on television, or on the playground. It must be explicitly taught and practiced. One unique challenge to teachers of English learners is that students learning English may arrive in our schools for the first time in any grade level, not just in kindergarten. This means that at every grade level, teachers need to be prepared with a tool kit of strategies to accelerate language learning and to backfill skills that may have been taught and mastered by other students in previous grade levels.

Another challenge is that some students arrive with high levels of mathematics preparation from their home country. These students may know the mathematics, but now must learn the subject matter discourse in order to ask questions, read and comprehend the textbook, and otherwise participate in class.

Real Math is innovative in its approach to recognizing and systematically developing academic language in the area of mathematics.

Language Mini Lessons

Many *English Learner Support Guide* pages begin with a language mini lesson that directly supports the concepts and skills being taught in that lesson. It takes into account that English learners may not yet have learned English vocabulary and structures that English-speaking students of that same grade level have acquired and do not need to be taught. These mini lessons focus on several areas of language development, including vocabulary, syntax, and grammar. These mini lessons give English learners a stronger language base for developing the skills in each lesson.

Access Vocabulary

In addition to the specialized terminology of mathematics, academic language often includes the use of common English idiomatic expressions and content-area words that have multiple meanings in English. Previewing these expressions with English learners and helping them keep track of their usage and meaning is excellent practice for extending knowledge of English for academic purposes.

In each **Real Math** lesson several words or expressions are noted along with a quick description of their meaning. Some of the words and expressions are math phrases, but many are examples of wider vocabulary used in word problems and direction lines in the lessons. For example, in a lesson on money, English learners will hear expressions that may be completely new to them. These are key to a deeper understanding of the lesson, although they are words that English speakers probably know. The Access Vocabulary highlights some of these key phrases and gives teachers a brief explanation. In this way, teachers do not have to preview every page, but can still focus on providing access to the same core lesson through comprehensible input for English learners.

The inclusion of Access Vocabulary, such as the double-meaning words that students encounter in the subject area, brings to the attention of teachers those complexities that English speakers may already have mastered but that can make the difference between deep comprehension and confusion for English learners. Access Vocabulary also highlights some potentially puzzling idiomatic expressions and recommends that teachers help students collect these in a phrase book or word bank to refer to for greater understanding. In order to help students learn some of these expressions and idiomatic phrases, teachers can introduce them before the lesson begins, or highlight them as they come up in the lesson.

Example:

Tally marks SE p. 14	small, written marks corresponding to some action or count of objects used to keep track of wins and losses
Keep track SE p. 15	use of a chart to write each result so as not to forget
Heads and tails TE p. 14B	Each side of a U.S. coin has a *head,* or picture of a famous person's face, and a *tail,* which is the back side of the coin. Currently, the U.S. Federal Reserve is putting different pictures on the tail or "flip" side of the U.S. quarters and nickels.

Cognates

One way to rapidly accelerate the acquisition of more sophisticated academic language is to take advantage of words with shared roots across languages. Words that are related by root or are borrowed from another language are called *cognates*. In English, many math and science terms come from Greek, Latin, and Arabic roots. English learners who speak Romance languages like Spanish have a wonderful advantage in these subjects because much of the important concept vocabulary is so similar in both languages. By teaching students to look for some basic word parts in English, these students can take advantage of what they know in their primary language to augment their knowledge of English. Pronunciation of these words may be quite different, but the written words often look very similar and mean the same thing.

In each language that shares cognates with English, there are also a few *false cognates*. These are words that look like they are the same in both languages, but actually mean something quite different. For example, English and Spanish share the word *actual,* but in Spanish the word means "nowadays," and in English it means "real."

Throughout the **English Learner Support Guide,** we highlight several key Spanish cognates in each lesson, as well as include a cumulative list of all the Spanish/English cognates for the grade-level span. Teachers may want to create a word wall to capture these math-related cognates, and have students keep a word book of cognates, as well as teach the cognate patterns to rapidly improve their English vocabulary. Keeping a list of any false cognates can be fun and useful.

Many languages share cognates with English, and there are a variety of resources available to use in the same way we have modeled the use of Spanish/English cognates. For example, by entering "cognates" in your Internet search engine, you can find a number of languages referenced.

See the Appendix for a list of English/Spanish cognates.

Sheltered Instruction

When English learners work in the core-content areas, they face the challenge of both the new concept load and the new language load. Sheltered Instruction designs lesson delivery to take advantage of student language strengths and techniques that do not rely solely on telling, but on doing so that students see, hear, and experience the new concept along with the new language. *Real Math* employs the following sheltered instruction strategies throughout the program.

Accessing Prior Knowledge Sheltered Instruction begins with **accessing students' prior knowledge** to determine what they already know and how much background building may be necessary. The lessons in *Real Math* begin with Mental Math exercises and then discussions and activities that provoke students to think about and share what they already know, allowing the teacher to diagnose where any gaps may exist.

Modeling the new math skills and concepts is a huge part of *Real Math,* and it is one of the key strategies involved with Sheltered Instruction. When we introduce new skills and concepts, they are built on prior learning and students see their teacher demonstrate using manipulatives, hear the appropriate language terminology modeled, and practice in a guided setting.

Checking for Understanding Sheltered Instruction involves interaction with the teacher, including **checking for understanding** along the way. When students are in the early stages of English language acquisition, they may not always be the first to answer a question or be able to fully express their ideas in speech or in writing. *Real Math* builds in many modes of checking comprehension throughout the lesson so that all students can show what they know. For example, a lesson may suggest that students use a signal, such as thumbs-up or thumbs-down, to indicate their understanding. In this way, English learners access the core concepts but do not have to rely only on English expression to show what they know or where they need additional help.

Explicit Instruction The step-by-step instruction in *Real Math* is carefully structured to lead students to understanding the concepts. Built into the teaching are explanations of new terms and skills. It provides for plenty of repetition and revisiting of these concepts using the new language so that students have plenty of modeling before they are expected to use these terms themselves.

Math Games English learners need to practice their new language in authentic settings rather than with drills that do not capture the language tasks students need to perform in school. Language learning can be a high-anxiety experience because the nature of the learning means that the speaker will make many mistakes. This can be profoundly difficult in front of one's peers or in answering individual questions in front of the whole class. Working in pairs and groups allows English learners a way to understand in a low-anxiety environment and allows more learning to take place.

A big part of the practice built into *Real Math* is in the form of learning games. In addition to being fun and motivating, math games provide English learners ample opportunity to practice their English while practicing their math. The *Real Math* games provide plenty of meaningful practice. Vocabulary is woven into appropriate language repetition and revisiting skills and strategies. In turn, students bring these games home, which draws the family into the practice of English. In addition, these specially designed games model strategic thinking so that even students at beginning levels of proficiency learn strategy and can demonstrate strategic, higher-level thinking.

Preview/Review Technique

Sheltered-content lessons are taught in English using many of the techniques described in this guide. In order to make sure that students deeply comprehend the concepts in each lesson, this guide also provides for the effective use of students' primary language using a model called *Preview/Review*. The core math lesson is taught to the entire class in English, using sheltered techniques.

After the core-sheltered lesson is taught, a quick review of the key concepts in the primary language allows students to converse with peers who speak the same primary language to be sure concepts are clear. If the teacher or an aide speaks the primary language of the students, this provides the additional benefit of answering questions and elaborating on the key concepts for students.

One of the true benefits of Preview/Review is that students focus on the lesson in English rather than waiting for the primary language translation to alternate in. In this guide, the Preview/Review is provided in Spanish and English. For classrooms where other languages are spoken, the teacher can use the English model as an example of what the primary language preview would include.

Estimating

Preview Key Ideas

Briefly preview the key ideas of the lesson in the students' primary language so that pupils can better comprehend English instruction.

En esta lección aprendemos que se puede hacer un estimado más exacto cuando contamos una parte de la cantidad y usamos los datos para ayudarnos a formar nuestra opinión.	In this lesson we learn that we can make a more accurate estimate when we count some part of the quantity and use that information to help us form our opinion.

Access Vocabulary

Before or during the lesson, be sure to clarify the terms below:

good chance (*Student Edition* p. 4) a good possibility, good probability based on odds rather than skill
altogether (*Student Edition* p. 5) total
actual answer (*Student Edition* p. 4) precise answer rather than estimated amount

Spanish Cognates

These words take advantage of what students and their families may know in their home language in order to accelerate the acquisition of math concepts in English.

to estimate estimar
approximately aproximadamente

Review Key Ideas

Have students complete the activity below to make sure that they understand the lesson concept. Divide students into groups and provide each group with a container filled with objects.

Con tus compañeros observen un recipiente de objetos y hagan una estimación de la cantidad. Describan o dibujen un diagrama del proceso que usaron para decidir el número estimado.	In groups, look at the container of objects and estimate the number of objects in the container. Discuss with your group how you came up with the number for your estimate. Describe or draw a diagram of the process your group used.

Place Value

Preview Key Ideas

Briefly preview the key ideas of the lesson in the students' primary language so that pupils can better comprehend English instruction.

Debido al valor de posición, los mismos dígitos pueden representar números diferentes. Por ejemplo, un 2 y un 4 pueden formar 24 ó 42. En esta lección usarás los mismos dígitos para formar números mayores y menores. Vamos a practicar esta destreza con el Roll a Number Game.	Due to place value, the same digits can represent different numbers. For example, a 2 and a 4 can form 24 or 42. In this lesson we will use the same digits to form greater and lesser numbers. We will practice this skill with the **Roll a Number Game.**

Access Vocabulary

Before or during the lesson, be sure to clarify the terms below:

draws slips (*Teacher's Edition Vol 1* p. 8B) pulls papers from a container; Here the word *draw* does not mean to illustrate or make a picture.
greatest (*Student Edition* p. 10) most, largest, or highest value; In this context *greatest* does not mean wonderful.
Roll a Number Game (*Teacher's Edition Vol 1* p. 8B) a *Real Math* game used to practice math and using a *Number Cube*

Spanish Cognates

These words take advantage of what students and their families may know in their home language in order to accelerate the acquisition of math concepts in English.

digits dígitos
mathematical matemático
practice práctica
value valor

Review Key Ideas

Have students complete the activity below to make sure they understand the lesson concept.

¿Qué información se puede usar para indicar cuál número es más grande que otro? *Con tu pareja, describe las claves que puedes usar.*	Describe what quick shortcuts you can use to tell which number is greater than another.

Numerical Sequence

Preview Key Ideas

Briefly preview the key ideas of the lesson in the students' primary language so that pupils can better comprehend English instruction.

En esta lección repasamos la sucesión numérica. Vamos a ver que a veces es más útil contar hacia adelante y otras veces es mejor contar hacia atrás. Describe una situación donde necesitemos contar hacia atrás. [contar el tiempo que queda en un partido de fútbol americano o de baloncesto] Describe una situación donde necesitemos contar hacia adelante. [contar dinero contar días en el calendario] Jugaremos el Order Game para tener más práctica.	In this lesson we will review numerical sequence. We will see that sometimes it is more useful to count on and other times it is better to count back. Describe a situation where we need to count back. [Possible answer: counting the time left in a football or basketball game] Describe a situation where we need to count on. [Possible answer: to count money or count days on the calendar] We will play the **Order Game** for more practice.

Access Vocabulary

Before or during the lesson, be sure to clarify the terms below:

count on (*Student Edition* p. 12) count by increasing by 1 each time (5, 6, 7, 8, 9, and so on)
count back (*Student Edition* p. 12) count by decreasing the number by 1 each time (10, 9, 8, 7, 6, 5, 4, and so on)
missing numbers (*Student Edition* p. 12) numbers absent from an equation or pattern; sometimes called the *unknown*
order (*Student Edition* p. 13) order means a sequence, not a random arrangement

Spanish Cognates

These words take advantage of what students and their families may know in their home language in order to accelerate the acquisition of math concepts in English.

order orden
probability probabilidad
sequence secuencia

Review Key Ideas

Have students complete the activity below to make sure they understand the lesson concept.

Nombren tres diferentes maneras de contar nuestra vida cotidiana aquí en la escuela. ¿Cuál usamos más, contar hacia delante o contar hacia atrás? ¿Por qué piensas así?	Name three different uses for counting in our daily lives here at school. Which do we use more commonly, counting on or counting back? Why do you think so? [Possible answer: We use counting on more often. When we need to track something, we don't always know the end point so we start at one point and count on.]

Rounding

Preview Key Ideas

Briefly preview the key ideas of the lesson in the students' primary language so that pupils can better comprehend English instruction.

No siempre se necesita un número preciso. A veces nada más necesitamos saber más o menos cuántos. Piensa en algunas situaciones donde se necesita un número exacto y otras cuando no.	Sometimes we need a precise number. Other times we just need to know more or less how many. Think about some situations which require an exact number and others which don't require an exact number. [Possible answer: Pharmacists need to know an exact number when writing prescriptions. A person needs to know more or less how much food to prepare for a party.]

Access Vocabulary

Before or during the lesson, be sure to clarify the word and phrase below:

reasonable approximation (*Student Edition* p. 15) not extreme or excessive, using common sense
about how many (*Teacher's Edition Vol 1* p. 14B) approximately, not asking for a precise number answer

Spanish Cognate

This word takes advantage of what students and their families may know in their home language in order to accelerate the acquisition of math concepts in English.

computation computación

Review Key Ideas

Have students complete the activity below to make sure they understand the lesson concept.

Dibuja una situación donde sería apropiado redondear números. Practica describiendo estás cantidades usando éstas frases: La _____ es aproximadamente _____ o la _____ es sobre _____.	Draw a picture of a situation where it is appropriate to round numbers for convenience. Practice describing this quantity by using the phrase, *The _____ is approximately _____ or the _____ is about _____.*

Practicing Addition and Subtraction

Preview Key Ideas

Briefly preview the key ideas of the lesson in the students' primary language so that pupils can better comprehend English instruction.

En esta lección mostramos la ecuación en diferentes estilos. A veces la suma empieza la ecuación. En otra, termina la ecuación. La posición de la suma no afecta el valor. Leemos la ecuación 9 = 4 + 5. La letra n representa el número incógnito.	In this lesson the number sentences are displayed in different ways. Sometimes the sum begins the number sentence. In others it ends the number sentence. The position of the sum does not make any difference in the value. We read the number sentence by saying, 9 = 4 + 5.

Access Vocabulary

Before or during the lesson, be sure to clarify the term and phrase below:

figure out the number (*Student Edition* p. 17) work out the problem to determine the number
hardest fact (*Student Edition* p. 17) most difficult fact

Spanish Cognates

These words take advantage of what students and their families may know in their home language in order to accelerate the acquisition of math concepts in English.

addition adición
subtraction sustracción
kilometers kilómetros

Review Key Ideas

Have students complete the activity below to make sure they understand the lesson concept. Divide students into groups.

¿Cuáles de las operaciones son las más difíciles para recordar? Comparte con tu grupo tus sugerencias para recordar bien las operaciones.	Which addition and subtraction facts do you have the hardest time remembering? Share with the group your suggestions for remembering the facts quickly.

Function Machines

Preview Key Ideas

Briefly preview the key ideas of the lesson in the students' primary language so that pupils can better comprehend English instruction.

En esta lección vamos a continuar a trabajar con funciones. Vamos a trabajar con máquinas de funciones donde no sabemos la regla, nada más sabemos la entrada y la salida. Veremos como se determina la regla con esta información.	In this lesson we are going to continue to work with functions. We are going to work with function machines where we don't know what the rule is, only the input and the output. We will see how we can determine the rule from this information.

Access Vocabulary

Before or during the lesson, be sure to clarify the phrase below:

act out the stories (*Student Edition* p. 24) demonstrate the action described in the story
spent (*Student Edition* p. 24) irregular past tense of spend

Spanish Cognates

These words take advantage of what students and their families may know in their home language in order to accelerate the acquisition of math concepts in English.

function función
complete completa
attention atención

Review Key Ideas

Have students complete the activity below to make sure they understand the lesson concept. Divide students into groups.

Con tus compañeros hagan una máquina de funciones. Describe como la máquina trabaja con números. Enseña tu máquina de funciones a otros grupos para descubrir la regla.	Describe how function machines work with numbers. Make a function machine. Show the others in your group, and have them try to solve it.

Missing Addends

Preview Key Ideas

Briefly preview the key ideas of the lesson in the students' primary language so that pupils can better comprehend English instruction.

En esta lección jugamos el juego de Números en las Espaldas. Observa el número de tu compañero, pero no veas el tuyo. Tus otros compañeros pueden ver los dos números. ¿Cuál es la suma de los dos números? Uds. dos deben decidir qué número tienen colocado en la espalda. Hacen preguntas para adivinar el número que traes puesto.	In this lesson we will play **Numbers on the Back**. You may look at your partner's number, but you may not look at your own. You can ask for the sum of the two numbers. You and your partner have to decide what numbers you have on your backs. Ask for clues in order to figure out your number.

Access Vocabulary

Before or during the lesson, be sure to clarify the words below:

difference (*Student Edition* p. 27) the amount that remains after one quantity is subtracted from another or the amount by which one quantity is greater or less than another
sum (*Student Edition* p. 27) Many English speakers have learned in earlier grades that sum means *total*. Help students know that sum is different in concept and spelling to *some*. In Spanish the word sum is *suma*.
sheets (*Teacher's Edition Vol 1* p. 26B) pieces of paper

Spanish Cognates

These words take advantage of what students and their families may know in their home language in order to accelerate the acquisition of math concepts in English.

equation ecuación
difference diferencia

Review Key Ideas

Have students complete the activity below to make sure they understand the lesson concept. Divide students into groups.

Juega el **Numbers on the Back Game** *con tu grupo de compañeros. Usa unas preguntas básicas para descubrir el número en tu espalda cómo: ¿Cuál es el número en la espalda de mi compañero? ¿Cuál es la suma de nuestros números?*	Play the **Numbers on the Back Game** with a group. Use some basic questions to discover the number on your back, such as the following: *What is the number on my partner's back? What is the sum of our numbers?*

Perimeter

Preview Key Ideas

Briefly preview the key ideas of the lesson in the students' primary language so that pupils can better comprehend English instruction.

En esta lección aprendemos que el perímetro de una figura es la distancia a su alrededor. Para hallar el perímetro sumas la medida de cada lado. Vamos a ver diferentes situaciones en que se necesita medir el perímetro.	In this lesson we learn that the perimeter of a shape is the length of the path around it. In order to find the perimeter we add the measurement of each side. We will also see different situations where we need to measure perimeter.

Access Vocabulary

Before or during the lesson, be sure to clarify the terms below:

cm (*Student Edition* p. 30) symbol for the word *centimeter*
figure (*Student Edition* p. 30) Here the word *figure* is used to refer to a geometric shape.

Spanish Cognates
These words take advantage of what students and their families may know in their home language in order to accelerate the acquisition of math concepts in English.

determine determina
figure figura
perimeter perímetro
centimeters centímetros
diagrams diagramas
rectangle rectángulo
equilateral equilátero
triangle triángulo

isosceles isósceles
equal igual
congruent congruente
area área
line línea
segments segmentos
park parque

Review Key Ideas

Have students complete the activity below to make sure they understand the lesson concept. Divide students into pairs.

Con tu compañero(a), dibujen dos ejemplos de situaciones donde se necesitarían saber el perímetro. No se olviden incluir la medida de cada lado.	With a partner, draw two situations where we would need to know the perimeter. Don't forget to include the measurements for each side.

Using Maps and Charts

Preview Key Ideas

Briefly preview the key ideas of the lesson in the students' primary language so that pupils can better comprehend English instruction.

En esta lección el trabajo es practicar a solucionar problemas usando datos de una tabla. También nos va presentar conjuntos de muchos objetos y vamos a trabajar a eliminar selecciones que no son la solución a un problema dado.	In this lesson we practice solving problems using data from a table. We will work to eliminate answer choices that are not the correct answer to the problem.

Access Vocabulary

Before or during the lesson, be sure to clarify the term below:

km (*Teacher's Edition Vol 1* p. 32B) symbol for kilometer

Spanish Cognates

These words take advantage of what students and their families may know in their home language in order to accelerate the acquisition of math concepts in English.

kilometer kilómetro
distance distancia
population población
map mapa
table tabla
chart gráfico
algorithm algorítmo
census censo
percent porciento
proportion proporción

Review Key Ideas

Have students complete the activity below to make sure they understand the lesson concept.

Con tu compañero(a), busca los datos de la población de la ciudad en donde vives. Compárala con las ciudades de la tabla en la lección 1.9 de tu libro. Luego responde las siguientes preguntas: ¿Cuántos viven en tu ciudad? ¿La población de tu ciudad es mayor o menor que la población de las ciudades listadas en la lección 1.9? Escribe el nombre de tu ciudad junto con los datos de su población.	With a partner, find the population of the city in which you live and compare it to the cities listed on the chart in your **Student Edition** Lesson 1.9. Then answer the following questions: What is the population in your city? Is it greater than or less than the cities listed in Lesson 1.9? Write the name of your city and the population.

Multidigit Addition

Preview Key Ideas

Briefly preview the key ideas of the lesson in the students' primary language so that students can better comprehend the English instruction.

En esta lección practicaremos a sumar números polidígitos. Sumar números polidígitos es similar a la suma que haz hecho hasta ahora. Cuando sumas números polidígitos, comienza a sumar por la derecha porque así es más fácil de reagrupar.	In this lesson we will practice adding multidigit numbers. Adding multidigit numbers together is similar to the addition we have done so far. When adding multidigit numbers, begin on the right because it is easier to regroup.

Access Vocabulary

Before or during the lesson, be sure to clarify the terms below:

shortcut (*Student Edition* p. 49) a quicker way of arriving at an answer by using fewer steps
calories (*Student Edition* p. 48) a measurement of the amount of energy in food
missing-term exercises (*Teacher's Edition Vol 1* p. 48B) mathematical equations where one part of the equation is missing

Spanish Cognates

These words take advantage of what students and their families may know in their home language in order to accelerate the acquisition of math concepts in English.

column columna
methods métodos
sum suma
mathematical reasoning razonamiento matemático
example ejemplo
calories calorías
multidigit multi dígito

Review Key Ideas

Have students complete the activity below to make sure that they understand the lesson concept. Have students work in pairs.

Con tu compañero(a) haz un póster para mostrar que pasaría si sumamos números polidígitos por la izquierda y no por la derecha. Muestren un ejemplo de una suma correcta y otro ejemplo de una suma incorrecta usando números polidígitos. Escriban los pasos en cada ejemplo.	With a partner, make a poster to show what can happen if you begin to add multidigit numbers on the left instead of the right. Show one example of correct addition of multidigit numbers and one example of incorrect addition of multidigit numbers. Label the steps in both examples.

Multidigit Subtraction

Preview Key Ideas

Briefly preview the key ideas of the lesson in the students' primary language so that students can better comprehend the English instruction.

En esta lección practicaremos a restar números polidígitos. Posiblemente necesitarás reagrupar cuando restes. No te olvides de comenzar a restar por la derecha porque es más fácil de reagrupar.	In this lesson we will practice subtracting multidigit numbers. When subtracting, we may need to regroup. We will begin on the right because it is easier to regroup.

Access Vocabulary

Before or during the lesson, be sure to clarify the words and phrase below:

rest (*Student Edition* p. 52) Here the word *rest* means "the number left over after subtraction takes place."
regroup (*Student Edition* p. 52) to group again; the prefix *re-* means "to do again"
reroll (*Student Edition* p. 55) to roll again
kept track of the money (*Student Edition* p. 54) wrote down the money to have a record

Spanish Cognates

These words take advantage of what students and their families may know in their home language in order to accelerate the acquisition of math concepts in English.

the rest el resto
case caso
group grupo
differences diferencias

Review Key Ideas

Have students complete the activity below to make sure that they understand the lesson concept. Have students work in small groups. The **Roll a Problem Game** is located in the *Student Edition* on page 55.

Después de jugar el Roll a Problem Game, discute con tu grupo cuál prefieres jugar, la adición o la sustracción. Haz un gráfico de dos columnas. Indica con marcas de conteo cuántos del grupo prefieren la adición y cuántos la sustracción.	Play the **Roll a Problem Game.** Discuss whether you prefer playing the game with addition or subtraction. Make a two-column chart and use tally marks to record how many students in your group prefer addition and how many prefer subtraction.

Multidigit Addition and Subtraction

Preview Key Ideas

Briefly preview the key ideas of the lesson in the students' primary language so that students can better comprehend the English instruction.

En esta lección usarás lo que aprendiste acerca de la suma y la sustracción para completar ejercicios y resolver problemas. Tú puedes usar la suma y la sustracción en varias situaciones.	In this lesson we will use what we have learned about addition and subtraction to complete exercises and solve problems. We can use addition and subtraction in various situations.

Access Vocabulary

Before or during the lesson, be sure to clarify the terms and phrase below:

length (*Student Edition* p. 57) measurement for how long something is
word problems (*Student Edition* pp. 58–59) math problems that pose a situation
algorithm (*Student Edition* p. 56B) a set of rules for solving a math problem
Which stamps make exactly 55 cents? (*Student Edition* p. 58) Here the word *make* is used to mean "total."

Spanish Cognates

These words take advantage of what students and their families may know in their home language in order to accelerate the acquisition of math concepts in English.

algorithm algorítmo
distance distancia
diameter diámetro
table tabla
sphere esfera

Review Key Ideas

Have students complete the activity below to make sure that they understand the lesson concept.

Dibuja los planetas en orden con un tamaño y distancia relativa al sol. Discute las estrategias que usaste para resolver los problemas acerca de los planetas.	Draw the planets in order with relative size and distance from the sun. Discuss the strategies you used to solve the problems about the planets.

Using Relation Signs

Preview Key Ideas

Briefly preview the key ideas of the lesson in the students' primary language so that students can better comprehend the English instruction.

Hoy practicaremos usando signos relacionados para comparar números, sumas y diferencias. Los signos de desigualdad se usan para mostrar cuál de los dos valores es mayor. El lado abierto de el signo de desigualdad, indica que el valor es mayor que y la punta indica que el valor es menor que. El signo de igualdad se usa para mostrar que dos números son iguales.	Today we will practice using relation signs to compare numbers, sums, and differences. Inequality signs are used to show which of two values is greater. The open end of an inequality sign faces the greater value, and the pointed end of an inequality sign faces the smaller value. Equal signs are used to show that two values are the same.

Access Vocabulary

Before or during the lesson, be sure to clarify the terms below:

relation signs (*Teacher's Edition Vol 1* p. 60A) symbols that show how numbers relate to each other
less than (*Student Edition* p. 60) fewer than; smaller than
greater than (*Student Edition* p. 60) more than; Here the word *greater* means "larger."

Spanish Cognates

These words take advantage of what students and their families may know in their home language in order to accelerate the acquisition of math concepts in English.

relation relación
signs signos
zero cero
to compare comparar
inequality signs signos de desigualdad
2-digit 2 dígitos
sums sumas
differences diferencias

Review Key Ideas

Have students complete the activity below to make sure that they understand the lesson concept. Have students work in pairs. The **Inequality Game** is located in the *Student Edition* on page 61.

Con tu compañero(a) juega el juego llámado el Inequality Game que se encuentra situado en la página 61 de tu libro. Haz un gráfico con ejercicios de desigualdad e incluye tu propia explicación para cada ejercicio.	Play the **Inequality Game.** Make a chart with the inequality statements and include your own written explanation of each.

Addition and Subtraction with Hidden Digits

Preview Key Ideas

Briefly preview the key ideas of the lesson in the students' primary language so that students can better comprehend the English instruction.

Hoy usaremos todo lo que sabes acerca de los números. Resolverás problemas con números que faltan.	Today we will use what we already know about numbers to solve problems that have numbers with missing digits.

Access Vocabulary

Before or during the lesson, be sure to clarify the terms below:

missing digits (*Student Edition* p. 66) unknown numerals
hidden digits (*Student Edition* p. 66) unknown numerals
logical (*Teacher's Edition Vol 1* p. 66B) reasonably expected

Spanish Cognates

These words take advantage of what students and their families may know in their home language in order to accelerate the acquisition of math concepts in English.

possibly correct posiblemente correcto
logical inferences inferencias lógicas
to identify identificar
obviously wrong (incorrect) obviamente incorrecto
descriptions descripciones
techniques técnicas

Review Key Ideas

Have students complete the activity below to make sure that they understand the lesson concept. Have students work in pairs.

Con tu compañero(a) escoge dos problemas de tu libro. Escribe las descripciones y los pasos que usaste para resolver los problemas.	Choose two problems from *Student Edition* pages 66–67. Write descriptions or illustrate and label the steps you used to figure out the solutions.

Approximation Applications

Preview Key Ideas

Briefly preview the key ideas of the lesson in the students' primary language so that students can better comprehend the English instruction.

Hoy practicaremos a aproximar las respuestas a problemas reales. En algunas instancias una respuesta aproximada es más que suficiente.	Today we will practice approximating answers to real problems. In some instances, an approximate answer is good enough for the situation.

Access Vocabulary

Before or during the lesson, be sure to clarify the terms below:

mathematician (*Teacher's Edition Vol 1* p. 68B) an expert in mathematics
working through (*Student Edition* p. 68) complete a problem by using known methods or steps to find the answer
minted (*Student Edition* p. 69) made a coin
approximation (*Teacher's Edition Vol 1* p. 68A) an answer to a mathematical problem that is not precise but close enough for the purpose
called for (*English Learner Support Guide* p. 15) required or necessary
instances (*English Learner Support Guide* p. 15) examples; cases

Spanish Cognates

These words take advantage of what students and their families may know in their home language in order to accelerate the acquisition of math concepts in English.

approximation aproximación
calculation calculación
cumulative acumulativo
situation situación

Review Key Ideas

Have students complete the activity below to make sure that they understand the lesson concept. Have students work in small groups.

Trabaja con un grupo para hacer una lista de tres situaciones donde es mejor aproximar una solución y tres situaciones donde requiere una respuesta exacta. Explica por qué.	List three instances where it makes sense to approximate an answer and three instances where an exact answer is called for. Explain why.

Making Inferences

Preview Key Ideas

Briefly preview the key ideas of the lesson in the students' primary language so that students can better comprehend the English instruction.

Hoy vamos a practicar a aproximar sumas y diferencias. Algunas veces el dato que tenemos está incompleto. Para resolver los problemas estudiamos los hechos que tenemos y hacemos inferencias.	Today we are going to practice approximating sums and differences. Sometimes the data we have is incomplete. To solve problems, we study the facts we do have and make inferences.

Access Vocabulary

Before or during the lesson, be sure to clarify the words and phrase below:

survey (*Student Edition* p. 71) A survey is a list of questions we ask of many people to gather information or opinions.
estimate (*Student Edition* p. 71) a judgement based on available information
second half of the year (*Student Edition* p. 71) July through December

Spanish Cognates

These words take advantage of what students and their families may know in their home language in order to accelerate the acquisition of math concepts in English.

inferences inferencias
observing observando
reasoning razonando
conclusions conclusions
table tabla

Review Key Ideas

Have students complete the activity below to make sure that they understand the lesson concept. Divide students into groups and provide them with copies of surveys from the Internet.

Con tu grupo lee las encuestas de la Internet que tu maestro(a) les dió. Escriban preguntas para la encuesta acerca de un tema del cuál estén interesados. Haz la encuesta a tu clase y marca los resultados.	Read existing surveys. Write survey questions and choices about a topic in which you are interested. Conduct a survey of your classmates and tally the results.

Integers

Preview Key Ideas

Briefly preview the key ideas of the lesson in the students' primary language so that students can better comprehend the English instruction.

En esta lección vas a repasar los conceptos relacionados con números enteros positivos y números enteros negativos. Los números enteros positivos son números enteros mayores que cero y los números enteros negativos son números enteros menores que cero.	In this lesson you will review concepts related to positive and negative integers. Positive integers are whole numbers greater than zero, and negative integers are whole numbers less than zero.

Access Vocabulary

Before or during the lesson, be sure to clarify the terms below:

cm (*Teacher's Edition Vol 1* pp. 72–73) symbol for centimeter
positive (*Teacher's Edition Vol 1* p. 72B) more than zero
negative (*Teacher's Edition Vol 1* p. 72B) less than zero

Spanish Cognates

These words take advantage of what students and their families may know in their home language in order to accelerate the acquisition of math concepts in English.

refinery refinería
process proceso
natural natural
positive positivo
negative negativo
centimeter centímetro
golf golf
temperature temperatura

Review Key Ideas

Have students complete the activity below to make sure that they understand the lesson concept.

Discute acerca de las situaciones reales en que ves o usas números negativos, así como; el resultado en un partido de golf, temperaturas y yardas negativas en un juego de fútbol americano.	Discuss real-life examples in which you might see or use negative numbers, such as golf scores, temperatures, and negative yardage in football.

Adding and Subtracting Integers

Preview Key Ideas

Briefly preview the key ideas of the lesson in the students' primary language so that students can better comprehend the English instruction.

En esta lección practicarás a sumar y a sustraer números enteros. Para ayudarte a sumar y a sustraer números enteros vas a dibujar un dibujo usando dos colores diferentes o usando una línea numerada.	In this lesson we will practice adding and subtracting integers. Drawing pictures, using two different colored chips, or using a number line can help us figure out how to add and subtract integers.

Access Vocabulary

Before or during the lesson, be sure to clarify the terms below:

number line (*Student Edition* p. 74) a horizontal or vertical line with numbers written in order, at intervals

balance (*Student Edition* p. 75) the amount of money held in a bank account

Spanish Cognates

These words take advantage of what students and their families may know in their home language in order to accelerate the acquisition of math concepts in English.

calculators calculadoras
units unidades
model modelo
problem problema
to represent representar
parenthesis paréntesis

Review Key Ideas

Have students complete the activity below to make sure that they understand the lesson concept.

Crea o seleccionia dos problemas de la lección para mostrarlos sobre una línea numerada. Asegúrate de incluir por la menos un problema con sustracción de números negativos. Demuestra cómo obtuviste tu respuesta.	Create or select two problems from the lesson to show on a number line. Be sure to include at least one problem with subtraction of negative numbers. Demonstrate how you arrive at the answer.

Understanding Multiplication

Preview Key Ideas

Briefly preview key ideas of the lesson in the student's primary language so that students can better comprehend the English instruction.

Hay varios métodos de multiplicar números. Hoy vamos a practicar a multiplicar números usando el método de rejillas, la cuenta saltada y la adición repetida. También aprenderás que como la adición es conmutativa, también la multiplicación lo es. Nosotros podemos multiplicar números en cualquier orden y obtendremos el mismo producto.	There are different ways we can do multiplication. Today we will practice multiplication using the lattice method, skip counting, and repeated addition. We will also learn that, like addition, multiplication is commutative. We can multiply numbers in any order and get the same product.

Access Vocabulary

Before or during the lesson, be sure to clarify the terms below:

multiplication table (*Teacher's Edition Vol 1* p. 90A) Here the word table is a chart used to display multiplication facts.

left out (*Teacher's Edition Vol 1* p. 90–91) Many students know *left* as "the opposite of right." In this lesson, *left out* means "omitted" or "excluded" or "not used."

Spanish Cognates

These words take advantage of what students and their families may know in their home language in order to accelerate the acquisition of math concepts in English.

commutative conmutativa
concept concepto
to affect afectar
to omit omiter
to reduce reducir

Review Key Ideas

Have students complete the activity below to make sure that they understand the lesson concept.

Explica a tu compañero porque la sustracción y la división no son conmutativas. Incluye una resta y un problema de división para enseñar tu respuesta.	With a partner explain why subtraction and division are not commutative. Include a subtraction problem and a division problem in your answer.

Multiplying 0, 1, 2, and 10

Preview Key Ideas

Briefly preview key ideas of the lesson in the student's primary language so that students can better comprehend the English instruction.

Necesitamos saber cómo multiplicar con rapidez y sin errores. En esta lección hay algunas ideas que te pueden ayudar a llegar a esta meta. Por ejemplo, el multiplicar por 2 es igual que duplicar o sumar el número por sí mismo. El multiplicar por 1 quiere decir que tienes 1 de tal número, entonces el producto de 1 y ese número es el número. El multiplicar por 0 significa que no tomas ese número ni una vez entonces vale 0. Se escriben múltiplos de 10 con un 0 después del múltiplo en nuestro sistema. Cuatro veces diez son 40.	We need to know how to multiply quickly and accurately. In this lesson there are some ideas that can help us reach this goal. For example, multiplying by 2 is the same as doubling or adding the number to itself. Multiplying by 1 means that we have one of that number, so the product of 1 and that number is that number. Multiplying by 0 means that we never take that number, so it is worth 0. Multiples of 10 are written with a 0 after the multiple in our system. Four tens are 40.

Access Vocabulary

Before or during the lesson, be sure to clarify the word below:

product (*Student Edition* p. 93) the result of multiplying two or more numbers

Spanish Cognates

These words take advantage of what students and their families may know in their home language in order to accelerate the acquisition of math concepts in English.

product producto
to memorize memorizar
cumulative acumulativo

Review Key Ideas

Have students complete the activity below to make sure that they understand the lesson concept.

Trabaja en un grupo pequeño con compañeros que hablen tu mismo idioma para describir las reglas de la multiplicación cuando multiplicas por 0, 1, 2 y 10. Asegúrate que cada uno en tu grupo pueda explicar cada regla de la multiplicación para que así ayuden a los demás a entender los conceptos de la lección.	Work in small, like-language groups to describe the multiplication rules for multiplying by 0, 1, 2, and 10. Make sure that everyone in the group can explain every rule so that they understand the lesson concepts.

Multiplying by 5 and 9

Preview Key Ideas

Briefly preview key ideas of the lesson in the student's primary language so that students can better comprehend the English instruction.

En esta lección vemos que los múltiplos de 5 y 9 pueden ser recordados usando operaciones × 10. Mira la relación que existe entre los múltiplos pares de 5 y de 10. Para multiplicar un número por 5, puedes primero multiplicarlo por 10 y luego saca la mitad del producto. Para multiplicar un número por 9, multipla el número por 10 y luego sustrae ese número del producto.	In this lesson we see that the multiples of 5 and 9 can be remembered by using the × 10 facts. Look at the relationship between the even multiples of 5 and of 10. To multiply a number by 5, we multiply it by 10 and then take half of the product. To multiply a number by 9, we multiply the number by 10 and then subtract that number from the product.

Access Vocabulary

Before or during the lesson, be sure to clarify the phrases below:

half the product (*Student Edition* p. 94) half of the result of multiplying two or more numbers
odd and even numbers (*Student Edition* p. 94) Odd numbers are integers that, when divided by 2, always have a remainder of 1. When even numbers are divided by 2, they have no remainder.

Spanish Cognates

These words take advantage of what students and their families may know in their home language in order to accelerate the acquisition of math concepts in English.

to compare comparar
column columna
interior interior
to visit visitar
to form formar

Review Key Ideas

Have students complete the activity below to make sure that they understand the lesson concept.

Escribe una descripción del patrón que se forma cuando multiplicas por 9.	Write a description of the pattern formed when you multiply by 9.

Square Facts

Preview Key Ideas

Briefly preview key ideas of the lesson in the student's primary language so that students can better comprehend the English instruction.

Hoy vamos a aprender a encontrar el área de un cuadrado usando la multiplicación y aprenderemos acerca de las operaciones al cuadrado.	Today we will learn to find the area of a square using multiplication and learn about square facts.

Access Vocabulary

Before or during the lesson, be sure to clarify the words below:

figure (*Student Edition* p. 96) a visible shape or form
unit (*Student Edition* p. 96) a fixed quantity or size considered to be a standard of measurement
vending machine (*Teacher's Edition Vol 1* p. 96–97) a machine operated by inserting a coin into a slot, used for selling drinks, food, or other small items

Spanish Cognates

These words take advantage of what students and their families may know in their home language in order to accelerate the acquisition of math concepts in English.

interior interior
figure figura
area area
region región
experiment experimento
definition definición

Review Key Ideas

Have students complete the activity below to make sure that they understand the lesson concept.

Ayúdale a un(a) compañero(a) a que se aprenda las operaciones de multiplicación. Pregúntense varias operaciones de multiplicación. Pueden usar la tabla de multiplicar como una ayuda.	Help a classmate to learn the multiplication facts. Ask each other several multiplication facts. You may use the multiplication table if you need help.

Multiplying by 3, 4, 6, and 8

Preview Key Ideas

Briefly preview key ideas of the lesson in the student's primary language so that students can better comprehend the English instruction.

*Hoy repasamos la multiplicación por 3, 4, 6 y 8, y vamos a practicar la multiplicación con el **Multiplication Table Game**. En un repaso, practicamos las destrezas que ya aprendimos. Piensa bien en las estrategias que usamos para multiplicar los factores de 3, 4, 6, y 8.*	Today we will review multiplication by 3, 4, 6, and 8. We will also practice multiplication with the **Multiplication Table Game.** In a review, we practice skills we have already learned. Try to remember the strategies that we have used to multiply 3, 4, 6, and 8.

Access Vocabulary

Before or during the lesson, be sure to clarify the term and phrase below:

alternate method (*Teacher's Edition Vol 1* p. 98B) another way of doing something
to score as close to 100 as possible without going over (*Student Edition* p. 99) In this expression, *going over* means "to exceed." In this example, the goal is to score as close to 100 without exceeding 100.

Spanish Cognates

These words take advantage of what students and their families may know in their home language in order to accelerate the acquisition of math concepts in English.

to demonstrate demostrar
probability probabilidad

Review Key Ideas

Have students complete the activity below to make sure that they understand the lesson concept.

Quizá ya sabes esta cancioncita	You may know this song
2 y 2 son cuatro	2 + 2 is four
4 y 2 son seis	4 + 2 is six
6 y 2 son 8	6 + 2 is eight
Y 8 son, 16	And 8 is 16
Y 8 son 24	And 8 is 24
Y 8 son 32	And 8 is 32
Carlos va a la escuela y también voy yo.	Carlos goes to school and I go too.

Multiplication and Addition Properties

Preview Key Ideas

Briefly preview key ideas of the lesson in the student's primary language so that students can better comprehend the English instruction.

Ya sabemos la propiedad conmutativa que dice que el orden en el cual se multiplican dos números no altera el resultado. En esta lección trabajamos con otras dos reglas de la multiplicación que se puede usar en el Cube 100 Game. Usando la ley de la propiedad distributiva para encontrar la respuesta de 8 × 12, te darás cuenta que 8 × 10 es 80 y 8 × 2 es 16. El producto tiene que ser 80 + 16 = 96. También podemos escribir esta ecuación 8 × (10 + 2) = (8 × 10) + (8 × 2). Esta propiedad se llama la ley asociativa.	We already know the commutative law that says that the order in which we multiply two numbers does not change the result. In this lesson we work with two other multiplication rules that can be used for the **Cube 100 Game.** Using the distributive law to find the answer of 8 × 12, we know that 8 × 10 is 80 and 8 × 2 is 16. The product is 80 + 16 = 96. We can also write this equation 8 × (10 + 2) = (8 × 10) + (8 × 2). This is called the *associative law*.

Access Vocabulary

Before or during the lesson, be sure to clarify the words below:

commutative (*Student Edition* p. 100) relating to or designating a law stating that the sum or product of two or more quantities will be the same regardless of their order
identity elements (*Student Edition* p. 100) the numerals that can be used to determine the answer of missing-digit problems

Spanish Cognates

These words take advantage of what students and their families may know in their home language in order to accelerate the acquisition of math concepts in English.

identity identidad
associative asociativa
distributive distributiva
commutative conmutativa

Review Key Ideas

Have students complete the activity below to make sure that they understand the lesson concept.

Trabaja con tu compañero(a) para escribir unas ideas útiles acerca de los atajos 'shortcuts', o maneras de eliminar algunos pasos cuando resuelves problemas matemáticos. Den ejemplos de situaciones en que pudieran usar tales atajos 'shortcuts'.	Work together and write some useful ideas about shortcuts or ways to eliminate some steps when solving math problems. Give some examples of situations in which you can use these shortcuts.

Multiplying by 11 and 12

Preview Key Ideas

Briefly preview key ideas of the lesson in the student's primary language so that students can better comprehend the English instruction.

En esta lección aprendemos los patrones para multiplicar por 11 y por 12. Cada vez que el número 11 es añadido al dígito de unidades, entonces el dígito de decenas aumenta por uno. Podemos usar la adición con sumandos iguales para aprender las operaciones × 12.	In this lesson we learn the patterns for multiplying by 11 and 12. Each time 11 is added the ones digit and the tens digit are increased by one. We can use repeated addition to learn the × 12 facts.

Access Vocabulary

Before or during the lesson, be sure to clarify the terms and phrase below:

dozen (*Student Edition* p. 102) A *dozen* means the same as 12.
a gross is 12 dozen (*Student Edition* p. 102) The word *gross* is sometimes used to mean "unpleasant". Here *gross* is a quantity of 12 dozen things.
speed test (*Teacher's Edition Vol 1* p. 102) a test to improve speed and accuracy of math facts; the test taker competes against his or her own time, not against other test takers

Spanish Cognates

These words take advantage of what students and their families may know in their home language in order to accelerate the acquisition of math concepts in English.

quotient cociente
product producto
members miembros
champion campeón

Review Key Ideas

Have students complete the activity below to make sure that they understand the lesson concept.

Muestra lo que yá has aprendido acerca de la multiplicación por 11. Tú puedes escribir una descripción o usar una gráfica para mostrar tu respuesta.	Show what you have learned about multiplying 11. You may either write a description or use a graph to show your answer.

Estimating Area

Preview Key Ideas

Briefly preview key ideas of the lesson in the student's primary language so that students can better comprehend the English instruction.

Ya sabes como hallar el perímetro de un polígono, es decir la distancia alrededor. Sumas las longitudes de todos los lados. En esta lección practicamos a hallar el área de un rectángulo. Multiplicamos el largo por el ancho.	We already know how to find the perimeter of a polygon, that is, the distance around the figure. We add the length of every side. In this lesson we practice how to find the area of a rectangle. We multiply the length by the width.

Access Vocabulary

Before or during the lesson, be sure to clarify the terms below:

practical application (*Teacher's Edition Vol 1* p. 104A) putting the math skills into practice, using them in some real-life situation
easel (*Teacher's Edition Vol 1* p. 104–105) a standing frame or tripod used especially to hold an artist's canvas
actual (*Teacher's Edition Vol 1* p. 104–105) real or true; The term *actual* is a false Spanish cognate. In Spanish the term *actual* means "present day."

Spanish Cognates

These words take advantage of what students and their families may know in their home language in order to accelerate the acquisition of math concepts in English.

meter metro
area área
variation variación

Review Key Ideas

Have students complete the activity below to make sure that they understand the lesson concept.

Trabaja con tu compañero(a) para explicar cómo pequeñas variaciones de medida del largo o del ancho pueden impactar la medida del área.	Work together to explain how small variances in the length or width of a measurement can make a big difference in the area.

Finding Missing Factors

Preview Key Ideas

Briefly preview key ideas of the lesson in the student's primary language so that students can better comprehend the English instruction.

En esta lección trabajamos con la multiplicación cuando falta unos de los factores. Vas a jugar con tu compañero(a). Cada uno tiene un número en la espalda. No se pueden ver el número en su propia espalda. Puedes ver el de tu compañero(a). La clase les va a decir el producto de los dos factores. Con esta información puedes dividir el producto por el factor de tu pareja. Así vas a saber el factor en tu espalda.	In this lesson we will work on multiplication with a missing factor. We will play a game where two partners each have a number on their back. You will not be able to see your own number, but you can see the number on your partner's back and the class will tell you only the product of the two multiplicands. You then need to be able to figure out your number by dividing the total product by your partner's number. This will tell you the factor on your back.

Access Vocabulary

Before or during the lesson, be sure to clarify the terms below:

trips around (*Student Edition* p. 111) number of times traveled around something
missing-term problems (*Student Edition* p. 111) math problems that are missing numerals
mows the lawn (*Student Edition* p. 27) cuts grass with a machine
long-distance plan (*Student Edition* p. 113) a contract created in order to make phone calls from one location to another location that is far away

Spanish Cognates

These words take advantage of what students and their families may know in their home language in order to accelerate the acquisition of math concepts in English.

factor factor
expression expresión
to deposit depositar

Review Key Ideas

Have students complete the activity below to make sure that they understand the lesson concept.

Discute acerca del número cero en relación con el Missing Factor Game. ¿Por qué el número cero crea una especial dificultad en el Missing Factor Game?	Discuss the number zero in relation to the **Missing Factor Game**. Why does the number zero create a special difficulty in the **Missing Factor Game**?

Multiplication and Division

Preview Key Ideas

Briefly preview key ideas of the lesson in the student's primary language so that students can better comprehend the English instruction.

Hoy vamos a repasar la multiplicación y la división. También vamos a practicar ecuaciones que les falta un factor y vamos a aprender acerca de la relación entre la multiplicación y la división. Vas a jugar el **Missing Factor Game** *pero esta vez vas a escribir un enunciado de división con los números que tienes en las espaldas y el producto de esos números.*	Today we review the work we have been doing with multiplication and division. We will practice with missing-factor equations and will learn about the relationship between multiplication and division. We will play the **Missing Factor Game** but this time we will write a division sentence out of the numbers on our backs and the product of those numbers.

Access Vocabulary

Before or during the lesson, be sure to clarify the words and phrases below:

undoes (*Student Edition* p. 114) reverses what has been done; causes the opposite action
earned (*Student Edition* p. 114) to have received money in return for completed work
how much he makes each hour (*Student Edition* p. 114) Here *makes* refers to the amount of money that is paid for each hour that is worked.
The Hawks came from behind to win. (*Student Edition* p. 115) In this sentence, the team named the Hawks was losing but at the end of the game the Hawks won.
touchdown (*Student Edition* p. 115) a way of scoring 6 points in American football

Spanish Cognates

These words take advantage of what students and their families may know in their home language in order to accelerate the acquisition of math concepts in English.

quotient cociente
kilometers kilómetros

Review Key Ideas

Have students complete the activity below to make sure that they understand the lesson concept.

Trabaja independientemente, dibuja o dramatiza las situaciones en los problemas y revisa si tus respuestas tienen sentido.	Working independently, draw or act out the situations in the problems and check whether your answers make sense.

Division with Remainders

Preview Key Ideas

Briefly preview key ideas of the lesson in the student's primary language so that students can better comprehend the English instruction.

En esta lección vamos a ver que es un residuo y cómo se soluciona la situación de formar conjuntos o equipos iguales. Vamos a ver que en algunos casos el residuo no puede ser dividido más y en otras, sí.	In this lesson we are going to see what a remainder is and how we might solve a situation where we want to form equal-sized teams or sets and there is one or more extras. We will see that in some cases the remainder can be divided up further and in others it cannot.

Access Vocabulary

Before or during the lesson, be sure to clarify the terms below:

play money (*Teacher's Edition Vol 1* p. 116A) coins and bills that are printed to look like currency but is worthless and is intended to be used in games and practice situations

denominations (*Teacher's Edition Vol 1* p. 116B) Printed money comes in specific amounts, or "denominations." United States currency comes in $1, $2, $5, $10, $20, $50, $100, etc.

fund (*Teacher's Edition Vol 1* p. 116–117) A fund is a collection of money, usually kept in a bank.

driftwood (*Student Edition* p. 117) wood drifting on water or that has been washed ashore by water

Spanish Cognates

These words take advantage of what students and their families may know in their home language in order to accelerate the acquisition of math concepts in English.

divisor divisor
quotient cociente
dividend dividendo
denominations denominaciones
important importante
coral coral

Review Key Ideas

Have students complete the activity below to make sure that they understand the lesson concept.

Haz una lista de todas las maneras en las que pudiéras resolver el problema de un residuo.	Make a list of all the ways you could fairly resolve the issue of a remainder.

Common Multiples and Common Factors

Preview Key Ideas

Briefly preview key ideas of the lesson in the student's primary language so that students can better comprehend the English instruction.

En la operación de multiplicación, 3 × 6 = 18, el 3 y el 6 son factores de 18. Los factores son números que multiplicas para obtener el producto. Un múltiplo de un número es un número entero multiplicado por ese número. Los múltiplos de 3 son 3, 6, 9, 12, 15, 18,... Los múltiplos de 6 son 6, 12, 18, 24, 30,... Puedes llamar al 18 un múltiplo común de 3 y 6 porque es un múltiplo que tienen en común.	In the operation of multiplication 3 × 6 = 18, the 3 and the 6 are factors of 18. The factors are numbers that are multiplied in order to obtain the product. A multiple of a number is a whole number multiplied by that number. The multiples of 3 are 3, 6, 9, 12, 15, 18… The multiples of 6 are 6, 12, 18, 24, 30… We can call 18 a common multiple of 3 and 6 because it is a multiple that they have in common.

Access Vocabulary

Before or during the lesson, be sure to clarify the words below:

product (*Student Edition* p. 118) a number or algebraic expression obtained by multiplication
common (*Student Edition* p. 118) belonging equally to two or more; shared by all alike

Spanish Cognates
These words take advantage of what students and their families may know in their home language in order to accelerate the acquisition of math concepts in English.

common común
common factors factores comunes

Review Key Ideas

Have students complete the activity below to make sure that they understand the lesson concept.

Escribe los múltiplos de cada factor en una tabla. Encierren en un círculo los múltiplos comunes. Extiende las tablas si no hay ninguno. En algunos casos, el mínimo común múltiplo es uno de los factores por sí mismo. Por ejemplo: el mínimo común múltiplo de 3 y 6, es 6.	Write the multiples of each factor in a table. Circle the common multiples. If there are none, extend the tables. In some cases the least common multiple is one of the factors itself. For example, the least common multiple of 3 and 6 is 6.

Parentheses

Preview Key Ideas°

Briefly preview key ideas of the lesson in the student's primary language so that students can better comprehend the English instruction.

Hoy vamos a aprender el uso de los paréntesis en las matemáticas. Vamos a aprender que usamos paréntesis como una convención para conversar sobre las matemáticas más fácilmente. Vamos a ver que siempre hacemos la operación dentro de los paréntesis primero. De esta manera, nosotros haremos el problema de matemáticas en el mismo orden y la suma o producto será igual.	Today we are going to learn the use of parentheses in math. We are going to learn that we use parentheses as a convention in order to talk about math more easily. We will learn to do the operation that is inside the parentheses first. In this way, we all do the math problem in the same order and the sum or product will be the same.

Access Vocabulary

Before or during the lesson, be sure to clarify the word and phrase below:

predict (*Student Edition* p. 123) to announce a guess before knowing the answer
how parentheses led you to your answer (*Student Edition* p. 122) using what is known to explain how the parentheses work in a math problem to produce an answer
host (*Student Edition* p. 121) the person who invited everyone to the event

Spanish Cognates

These words take advantage of what students and their families may know in their home language in order to accelerate the acquisition of math concepts in English.

common factors factores comunes
parenthesis paréntesis
veterinarian veterinaria
conventions convenciónes

Review Key Ideas

Have students complete the activity below to make sure that they understand the lesson concept.

Trabaja con tu compañero(a) para decir la regla acerca de las operaciones entre paréntesis. Crea tres problemas narrativos en los que las respuestas requieran el uso de los paréntesis.	Work in pairs to tell the rule about the operations within parentheses. Create three word problems in which the solutions require the use of parentheses.

Applying Math

Preview Key Ideas

Briefly preview key ideas of the lesson in the student's primary language so that students can better comprehend the English instruction.

*En esta lección vamos a practicar aplicacando lo que ya hemos aprendido acerca de los paréntesis. Tendremos problemas que requieren que mostremos nuestro entendimiento de la convención o regla del uso del paréntesis y por qué los paréntesis dictan el orden en que hacemos las operaciones. También tendremos la oportunidad de jugar **Cubo** y a compartir la estrategia con los demás.*	In this lesson we will have practice in applying what we have learned about the basic operations and parentheses. We will have problems that require us to show that we understand the convention or rule of parentheses and why parentheses are used in determining the order in which we perform operations. We will also have the opportunity to play **Cubo** and check our strategy with others.

Access Vocabulary

Before or during the lesson, be sure to clarify the words below:

seedlings (*Student Edition* p. 124) young trees
perimeter (*Student Edition* p. 124) the length of the boundary of closed plane figure
scores (*Student Edition* p. 125) makes or gains points
paper route (*Student Edition* p. 124) a job of delivering newspapers
tree house (*Student Edition* p. 124) a platform or playhouse, usually for children, built in the branches of a tree

Spanish Cognates

These words take advantage of what students and their families may know in their home language in order to accelerate the acquisition of math concepts in English.

parentheses paréntesis
ranch rancho

Review Key Ideas

Have students complete the activity below to make sure that they understand the lesson concept.

Trabaja con tu compañero(a) para describir cómo tu sabes cuál operación usas para resolver un problema narrativo.	Work with partners to describe how you know which operation to use to solve a word problem.

Points on a Grid

Preview Key Ideas

Briefly preview the key ideas in the students' primary language so that students can better comprehend the English instruction.

En esta lección vas a trabajar con el mapa de una ciudad ficticia que se llama Graph City (Ciudad Gráfica). La ciudad está planificada para que las calles numeradas corran de norte a sur y que las avenidas numeradas corran de este al oeste. Así que es muy importante que sigas esta convención o regla, o puedes llegar a donde no quieres.	In this lesson we are going to work with the map of a fictional city called Graph City. The city is planned so the numbered streets run north and south while the numbered avenues run east and west. It is very important that we follow this numbering convention, or rule, or we could end up where we don't want to be.

Access Vocabulary

Before or during the lesson, be sure to clarify the terms below:

ordered pairs (*Student Edition* p. 142) pairs of numbers in which one of the pair is considered the first and the other the second
graph (*Teacher's Edition Vol 1* p. 140A) a diagram showing the changes of and the relationship between two or more things
horizontal (*Teacher's Edition Vol 1* p. 140B) parallel to level ground
vertical (*Teacher's Edition Vol 1* p. 140B) upright; a line going up and down

Spanish Cognates

These words take advantage of what students and their families may know in their home language in order to accelerate the acquisition of math concepts in English.

coordinates   coordenadas
intersection   intersección
graph   gráfica

Review Key Ideas

Have students complete the activity below to make sure that they understand the lesson concept. For this activity, divide students into groups and provide them with a copy of a map of your city that you have marked similarly to that in the *Student Edition* pages 141–142.

Junto con tu grupo mira el mapa de tu ciudad y contesta las siguientes preguntas: ¿Cuántas calles tiene tu Ciudad? ¿Y cuántas avenidas? ¿En dónde estuvieras en el Punto A? ¿Y en el Punto B? y así sucesivamente. ¿Alguno de éstos puntos se encuentra más de cuatro cuadras de distancia?	In your group, look at the city map and answer the following questions: How many streets are there? How many avenues are there? Where would you be at Point A? Point B? and so on. Are any of the points more than four blocks apart?

Coordinates

Preview Key Ideas

Briefly preview the key ideas in the students' primary language so that students can better comprehend the English instruction.

En esta lección vamos a practicar a localizar un punto usando dos coordenadas, y también vamos a determinar las coordenadas de un punto dado. Recuerden que un par de números ordenados también se llaman coordenadas. Y, que la convención estandardizada es siempre empezar los números ordenados con el horizontal y luego sigue el número vertical.	In this lesson, we will practice locating a point using two coordinates. We will also determine coordinates from a given point. Ordered pairs of numbers are also called coordinates and the standard convention is to always list the sideways, or horizontal, number first, and the up-down, or vertical, number second.

Access Vocabulary

Before or during the lesson, be sure to clarify the terms below:

homophone (*Student Edition* p. 143) words in English that sound exactly the same as another word, but are spelled and mean something different: no–know, pair–pear, two–to
given point (*Teacher's Edition Vol 1* p. 142A) a specific place on a chart
standard convention (*English Learner Support Guide* p. 34) most common tradition or way

Spanish Cognates
These words take advantage of what students and their families may know in their home language in order to accelerate the acquisition of math concepts in English.

vertical vertical
horizontal horizontal
angles ángulos
coordinates coordenadas

Review Key Ideas

Have students complete the activity below to make sure that they understand the lesson concept. Provide students with a coordinate grid similar to *Student Edition* page 143 but using different coordinates.

Usando una cuadrícula, haz una adivinanza o una pregunta para que tu compañero(a) la resuelva. Escribe la adivinanza en Inglés o en tu lengua nativa.	Using the coordinate grid, make up your own riddle or question for your partner to solve. Write the riddle in English or in your primary language.

Lengths of Lines on a Grid

Preview Key Ideas

Briefly preview the key ideas in the students' primary language so that students can better comprehend the English instruction.

En esta lección vamos a hallar longitudes de segmentos horizontales y verticales en una cuadrícula. También vamos a aprender a usar el Teorema de Pitágora para determinar longitudes de otros segmentos. El Teorema de Pitágora fué nombrado por un matemático griego Pitágoras.	In this lesson we will find the lengths of horizontal and vertical line segments on coordinate grids. We will use the Pythagorean Theorem to find lengths on a grid. The Pythagorean Theorem is named after the Greek mathematician Pythagoras.

Access Vocabulary

Before or during the lesson, be sure to clarify the term below:

right triangle (*Teacher's Edition Vol 1* p. 146B) In English the word *right* has many different meanings. It is the opposite of *wrong*, and it can be a direction—the opposite of left. A right triangle is a triangle with a right angle.

Spanish Cognates

These words take advantage of what students and their families may know in their home language in order to accelerate the acquisition of math concepts in English.

area área
segment segmento
distance distancia
to create crear
coordinates cordinas
to determine determinar

Review Key Ideas

Have students complete the activity below to make sure that they understand the lesson concept.

En una hoja de papel, dibuja diferentes clases de triángles y etiquétalos. Discute con tu compañero(a) de clase acerca de las características de un triángulo rectángulo.	On a sheet of paper, draw several different triangles and label them. Discuss with a like-language partner what characteristic makes the right triangle.

Function Rules

Preview Key Ideas

Briefly preview the key ideas in the students' primary language so that students can better comprehend the English instruction.

Cuando trabajas con reglas de funciones, es muy importante probarla con por lo menos dos ejemplos para asegurar que se aplica la regla a los dos.	When we work with function rules, it is very important to show that the rule works with at least two examples.

Access Vocabulary

Before or during the lesson, be sure to clarify the words below:

input (*Student Edition* p. 148) the information you put in the function machine
output (*Student Edition* p. 148) the information that comes out of the machine

Spanish Cognates
These words take advantage of what students and their families may know in their home language in order to accelerate the acquisition of math concepts in English.

total total
notation anotación
correct correcto
to represent representar
point punta
to pass pasar

Review Key Ideas

Have students complete the activity below to make sure that they understand the lesson concept.

Inventa una regla de funciones con 4 pares de números ordenados que vayan con tu regla de funciones.	Write a function rule, and show four pairs of numbers that could be generated by the rule.

Inverse Functions

Preview Key Ideas

Briefly preview the key ideas in the students' primary language so that students can better comprehend the English instruction.

En esta lección repasamos funciones inversos. Recuerda que la palabra inverso quiere decir lo contrario o lo opuesto. Por ejemplo, la división es lo inverso de la multiplicación.	In this lesson, we review inverse functions. The word *inverse* means "the opposite or reverse order." For example, division is the inverse of multiplication.

Access Vocabulary

Before or during the lesson, be sure to clarify the word and phrases below:

She made a total of $15. (*Student Edition* p. 152) The word *made* in this context means "earned."

undo (*Teacher's Edition Vol 1* p. 152B) reverse an action: This word is formed by adding the prefix *un-* to the word *do*. Inverse operations, like division and multiplication, undo the result of the other's action.

gives you back (*Teacher's Edition Vol 1* p. 152–153) returns; results in

Spanish Cognates

These words take advantage of what students and their families may know in their home language in order to accelerate the acquisition of math concepts in English.

inverse inverso
rectangular rectangular
basic básico
volunteer voluntario
to base on basar en
to suppose suponer

Review Key Ideas

Have students complete the activity below to make sure that they understand the lesson concept. Have students work in groups of two.

Con tu compañero(a), explica porque la multiplicación es la función inversa de la división. Dibuja un ejemplo para compartirlo con tu clase.	With your partner, discuss how multiplication is the inverse function of division. Draw an example to share.

Ordered Pairs

Preview Key Ideas

Briefly preview the key ideas in the students' primary language so that students can better comprehend the English instruction.

En esta lección vamos a jugar el **Function Game.** *También usaremos un código para solucionar acertijos. No te olvides que cualquier número multiplicado por 0 resulta en 0.*	In this lesson we will play the **Function Game.** We will use a code to solve riddles. Don't forget that any number multiplied by 0 will result in 0.

Access Vocabulary

Before or during the lesson, be sure to clarify the words below:

odd (*Student Edition* p. 155) *Odd* numbers are numbers that, when divided by 2, always have a remainder of one.
even (*Student Edition* p. 155) *Even* numbers are numbers that, when divided by 2, have no remainder.
score (*Student Edition* p. 157) to gain a point or points
round (*Student Edition* p. 157) A *round* in the **Function Game** refers to the completion of everyone's turn.
stool (*Teacher's Edition Vol 1* p. 157A) an individual seat supported on legs, usually having no back or arms
universal rule (*Teacher's Edition Vol 1* p. 157A) a rule that is shared by all or applies to everything

Spanish Cognate

This word takes advantage of what students and their families may know in their home language in order to accelerate the acquisition of math concepts in English.

pair par

Review Key Ideas

Have students complete the activity below to make sure that they understand the lesson concept. Have students play the **Function Game** in groups of two or more.

Juega el **Function Game** *con tus compañeros. Enseña al maestro o la maestro la regla de funciones que usabas y el resultado.*	Play the **Function Game,** then show me the rule you created and the outcome of the game.

Function Rules and Ordered Pairs

Preview Key Ideas

Briefly preview the key ideas in the students' primary language so that students can better comprehend the English instruction.

Ayer aprendímos que un par ordenado está formado de dos números escritos tal como uno está considerado antes que el otro. Coordenadas son puntos escritos como pares ordenados, con el eje x escrito primero, luego la coordenada y. Por ejemplo, (3, 4).	We have learned that *ordered pairs* are two numbers written so that one is considered before the other. Coordinates of points are written as ordered pairs, with the *x*-coordinate written first, then the *y*-coordinate (3, 4).

Access Vocabulary

Before or during the lesson, be sure to clarify the words below:

mile (*Student Edition* p. 158) In the sport of running, the *mile* is 4 times around a track.
ordered pair (*Teacher's Edition Vol 1* p. 158A) two numbers written so one is considered before the other; Coordinates of points are written as ordered pairs, with the *x*-coordinate written first and the *y*-coordinate second. An example is (2, 6).

Spanish Cognates

These words take advantage of what students and their families may know in their home language in order to accelerate the acquisition of math concepts in English.

to visualize visualizar
correct correcto
identity identidad
original original

Review Key Ideas

Have students complete the activity below to make sure that they understand the lesson concept.

Escribe por lo menos 4 pares ordenados para la función: *x* × 8.	Write at least four ordered pairs for the following function rule: *x* × 8.

Graphing Ordered Pairs

Preview Key Ideas

Briefly preview the key ideas in the students' primary language so that students can better comprehend the English instruction.

Hoy vas a ver que los pares ordenados pueden ser positivos o negativos. Veras que una cuadrícula tiene cuatro sectores creados por ejes.	Today we will see that ordered pairs can be positive or negative. We will also see that a grid has four sectors which are created by the axes.

Access Vocabulary

Before or during the lesson, be sure to clarify the word below:

ruler (*Student Edition* p. 160) A measuring stick that usually measures one foot in length and has smaller increment measurements such as inches, half inches, and centimeters.

Spanish Cognates

These words take advantage of what students and their families may know in their home language in order to accelerate the acquisition of math concepts in English.

calculations calculaciones
negative negativo
positive positivo
linear lineal
function función
sector sector
increment incremento

Review Key Ideas

Have students complete the activity below to make sure that they understand the lesson concept.

Usando por lo menos cuatro pares de ordenadas, grafica la función: $x + 4$. Discute con tu compañero(a) acerca de cómo te das cuenta si graficaste una función linear.	Using at least four ordered pairs, graph the following function: $x + 4$. Discuss with another student how you can tell if you graphed a linear function.

Identifying Scale

Preview Key Ideas

Briefly preview the key ideas in the students' primary language so that students can better comprehend the English instruction.

A veces los números que deseas representar en una gráfica parecen demasiado grandes para caber en una sola hoja cuadriculada. Hay una manera de hacer caber las coordenadas en tu papel cuadriculado. Puedes dejar que cada espacio represente más de una unidad.	Sometimes the numbers we want to represent on a graph may seem too large to fit on a single sheet of graph paper. There is a way to make the coordinates fit on the graph paper. We can make each space represent more than one unit of measure.

Access Vocabulary

Before or during the lesson, be sure to clarify the word and phrase below:

stands for (*Student Edition* p. 166) The phrase *stands for* means "represents."
increments (*Teacher's Edition Vol 1* p. 169A) measured, equal units
axis (*Teacher's Edition Vol 1* p. 166B) a straight, central line around which the parts of a figure are symmetrically arranged
create a skeleton (*Teacher's Edition Vol 1* p. 166B) In this phrase, the term *skeleton* means "outline" or "sketch". The author wants you to draw the graph without filling in any details.

Spanish Cognates

These words take advantage of what students and their families may know in their home language in order to accelerate the acquisition of math concepts in English.

temperature temperatura
scale escala
space espacio
unique único
value valor
specific específico

Review Key Ideas

Have students complete the activity below to make sure that they understand the lesson concept. Look through your local paper to find different graphs with different scales. Divide the students into small groups and give each group a graph.

Con tu grupo miren el gráfico que les dió la maestra o el maestro. Determinen la escala que fué usada y si la escala tiene sentido con la información del gráfico. Luego explica la escala de tu gráfico a toda tu clase.	In your group, look at the graph I gave you. Determine the scale that was used and if the scale makes sense for the information on the graph. Then explain the scale on your graph to the class.

Composite Function Rules

Preview Key Ideas

Briefly preview the key ideas in the students' primary language so that students can better comprehend the English instruction.

Recuerda que no todas las funciones tienen una gráfica representada con una recta. ¿Cuál sería un ejemplo de una función cuya gráfica no sea una recta? Un ejemplo es cuando la primer coordenada (la entrada) representa la longitud de un lado de un cuadrado y la salida representa el área del cuadrado: $y = x \times x = x^2$	Remember, not all functions have graphs that are straight lines. What would be an example of a function whose graph is not a line? One example is when the first coordinate (the input number) is the length of the side of a square and the output is the area of the square: $y = x \times x = x^2$

Access Vocabulary

Before or during the lesson, be sure to clarify the term below:

handling charge (*Student Edition* p. 172) an additional amount of money you pay that covers the cost of preparing the item

Spanish Cognates
These words take advantage of what students and their families may know in their home language in order to accelerate the acquisition of math concepts in English.

to combine combinar
public services servicios públicos
composite compuesto
final final
to offer ofrecer
additional adicional

Review Key Ideas

Have students complete the activity below to make sure that they understand the lesson concept.

Con un compañero haz tres ejemplos de funciones compuestas. No se olviden que una función compuesta emplea más que una operación.	Work in pairs to list three examples of composite functions. Remember that composite functions involve more than one operation.

Using Inverse Operations

Preview Key Ideas

Briefly preview the key ideas in the students' primary language so that students can better comprehend the English instruction.

Ya sabes de las funciones inversas. Hoy vamos a ver como se halla el inverso de una función compuesta. Recuerdas que una máquina de funciones −6 deshace el trabajo de una máquina de funciones +6. Es el inverso. También una máquina de ÷2 deshace el trabajo de una máquina de funciones ×2.	We have already learned about inverse functions. Today we are going to see how to find the inverse of a composite function. Remember that a −6 function machine undoes the work of a +6 function machine, and a ÷2 function machine undoes the work of a ×2 function machine.

Access Vocabulary

Before or during the lesson, be sure to clarify the term below:

shipping and handling fee (*Student Edition* p. 175) an additional amount of money you pay that covers the cost of preparing the item for shipping and the shipping charge itself

Spanish Cognates

These words take advantage of what students and their families may know in their home language in order to accelerate the acquisition of math concepts in English.

variables variables
to prepare preparar
ounce onza

Review Key Ideas

Have students complete the activity below to make sure that they understand the lesson concept. Have students work in small groups.

En tu grupo, expliquen cómo hallar un número desconocido en una máquina de funciones compuestas. Dibujen los pasos para enseñar a los demás como se hace.	Explain how you find an unknown number in a composite function machine. Draw the steps in order to show everyone else how to do it.

Graphing Composite Functions

Preview Key Ideas

Briefly preview the key ideas in the students' primary language so that students can better comprehend the English instruction.

Has representado gráficamente pares ordenados a partir de una sola regla de funciones. En esta lección vas a representar gráficamente pares ordenados a partir de funciones compuestas. No se olviden que una función compuesta incluye dos reglas de funciones.	We have graphed ordered pairs from one single function rule. In this lesson we are going to graph ordered pairs using composite functions. Remember that a composite function includes two function rules.

Access Vocabulary

Before or during the lesson, be sure to clarify the word and phrase below:

plot (*Teacher's Edition Vol 1* p. 176B) to follow the coordinates and mark the points on the graph
pick a point (*Student Edition* p. 177) To *pick a point* means "to select a specific place on a graph."
doorbell (*Teacher's Edition Vol 1* p. 176–177) a bell or buzzer on or near a door that is used by someone wanting to come in
ring (*Teacher's Edition Vol 1* p. 176–177) Many students may know the word *ring* to mean "jewelry worn on fingers". Here *ring* is a sound made by something like a bell.

Spanish Cognates

These words take advantage of what students and their families may know in their home language in order to accelerate the acquisition of math concepts in English.

relationship relación
to produce producir
intersection intersección
to visit visitar

Review Key Ideas

Have students complete the activity below to make sure that they understand the lesson concept.

Muestren cómo usar una gráfica para hallar pares ordenados.	Show how you use a graph to find ordered pairs.

Graphing Functions

Preview Key Ideas

Briefly preview the key ideas in the students' primary language so that students can better comprehend the English instruction.

Una vez que hayas usado una regla de funciones para calcular pares ordenados, puedes representarlos en una gráfica. En esta lección vamos a descubrir como hacer una gráfica. A ver que observas de las funciones cuando están representadas en la gráfica.	Once we have used a function rule to calculate ordered pairs, we can represent them on a graph. In this lesson, we are going to discover how to make a graph. Let's see what we observe about the functions when they are represented as a graph.

Access Vocabulary

Before or during the lesson, be sure to clarify the words and terms below:

function (*Student Edition* p. 178) a rule that uniquely defines how an independent variable relates to a dependent variable; every element of one set is <u>exactly</u> paired with an element of a second set

runway (*Teacher's Edition Vol 1* p. 178–179) a long, narrow strip of ground, along which something runs

stakes (*Teacher's Edition Vol 1* p. 178–179) sticks or posts sharpened at one end for driving into the ground

holds true (*Teacher's Edition Vol 1* p. 178B) continues to apply to; is still useable

Spanish Cognates

These words take advantage of what students and their families may know in their home language in order to accelerate the acquisition of math concepts in English.

element elemento
points puntos
problem problema
type (of paper) tipo (de papel)
distance distancia

Review Key Ideas

Have students complete the activity below to make sure that they understand the lesson concept. Divide the students into groups.

Hoy descubrimos la identidad de funciones. ¿Qué quiere decir eso? ¿Por qué sería que todas las gráficas de la misma función son iguales?	Today we learned about the identity function. With your group discuss this and write or draw a picture that explains the identity function. Explain why you think all graphs of the same function look the same.

Working with Graphs

Preview Key Ideas

Briefly preview the key ideas in the students' primary language so that students can better comprehend the English instruction.

Se puede representar en una gráfica los datos que juntamos en tablas. Una gráfica lineal es una línea que representa datos a lo largo de un período de tiempo.	We can represent on a graph the data we collect in tables. One very useful graph is a line graph which shows how data changes over time.

Access Vocabulary

Before or during the lesson, be sure to clarify the words below:

trends (*Student Edition* p. 180) the general direction in which things are changing
trial (*Student Edition* p. 180) In science, we conduct *trials* to try out ideas to see if they work. We may repeat the trials over and over with different numbers or substances or other variables to see if they still achieve the same results.
dormant (*Teacher's Edition Vol 1* p. 180B) temporarily inactive
sprout (*Teacher's Edition Vol 1* p. 180B) to begin to grow; develop or put forth young buds or growths

Spanish Cognates

These words take advantage of what students and their families may know in their home language in order to accelerate the acquisition of math concepts in English.

experiment experimento
results resultados
to germinate germinar
cumulative acumulativo

Review Key Ideas

Have students complete the activity below to make sure that they understand the lesson concept. Divide the students into groups.

Con tu grupo describe las dos gráficas que hizo Carlos y para que sirve cada una.	In your group, describe the two kinds of graphs Carlos made and the purpose each graph serves.

Misleading Graphs

Preview Key Ideas

Briefly preview the key ideas in the students' primary language so that students can better comprehend the English instruction.

Cuando estudias una gráfica es muy importante revisarla con cuidado. A veces unas gráficas están formadas para dar una impresión errónea. Es porque es posible representar datos en varias formas para enfatizar diferentes hechos.	When you read a graph, be sure to look at it carefully. Sometimes graphs are designed to give a first impression that is misleading. This is because it is possible to represent data in various forms in order to emphasize more different facts.

Access Vocabulary

Before or during the lesson, be sure to clarify the terms below:

impression (*Student Edition* p. 184) a perception based on a quick look or general description of the facts
profit graph (*Teacher's Edition Vol 1* p. 184–185) a diagram that displays income or financial gain and its relation to another factor such as sales
slope (*Teacher's Edition Vol 1* p. 184–185) the amount of the slant of a line on a graph
misled (*Teacher's Edition Vol 1* p. 184B) guided in the wrong direction; made to believe a wrong thought
significant (*Teacher's Edition Vol 1* p. 184–185) having special value or importance

Spanish Cognates

These words take advantage of what students and their families may know in their home language in order to accelerate the acquisition of math concepts in English.

analysis análisis
data datos
impression impresión
to indicate indicar

Review Key Ideas

Have students complete the activity below to make sure that they understand the lesson concept.

Describe las diferentes formas en que se representaron los datos en esta lección y cómo contribuía a una impresión errónea de la información.	Tell about different ways that data in this lesson was represented which contributed to a misleading impression of the information.

Multiplying by Powers of 10

Preview Key Ideas

Briefly preview the key ideas of the lesson in the students' primary language so that students can better comprehend the English instruction.

El producto de cualquier número y 10, está escrito con un 0 detrás del número. No decimos que añadimos cero al número. En realidad, multiplicas por 10 cuando escribes cero detrás del número. Por ejemplo, los números 10, 100, 1000, y 1,000,000,000 son potencias de 10. La regla general para multiplicar por números como 10, 100, y 1000 es contar cuántos ceros hay en la potencia de diez y escribir esta misma cantidad después del otro factor. Por ejemplo, 5 × 100 = 500	When we multiply some number of 10s together, we call the product a *power of ten*. For example, the numbers 10, 100, 1,000, and 1,000,000,000 are all powers of ten. The general rule for multiplying by numbers such as 10, 100, and 1,000 is to count how many zeros there are in the power of 10 and write that many zeros after the other factor. For example, two zeros are in the number 100. In the example 5 × 100, we write two zeros after the 5 to get 500; 5 × 100 = 500.

Access Vocabulary

Before or during the lesson, be sure to clarify the word and phrase below:

power of ten (*Student Edition* p. 200) the number of times 10 is multiplied by itself
shortcut (*Student Edition* p. 200) a way to solve a problem with fewer steps and less effort

Spanish Cognates
These words take advantage of what students and their families may know in their home language in order to accelerate the acquisition of math concepts in English.

sequence secuencia
metric system sistema métrico
result resultado

Review Key Ideas

Have students complete the activity below to make sure that they understand the lesson concept.

Haz una regla general para multiplicar por números como 10, 100, y 1,000.	Write a general rule for multiplying by numbers such as 10, 100, and 1,000.

Converting Metric Units

Preview Key Ideas

Briefly preview the key ideas of the lesson in the students' primary language so that students can better comprehend the English instruction.

Hoy vamos a practicar multiplicando potencias de diez para convertir números métricos.	Today we are going to practice multiplying by powers of ten to convert metric numbers.

Access Vocabulary

Before or during the lesson, be sure to clarify the terms below:

off guard (*Teacher's Edition Vol 1* p. 202B) not paying attention, not aware
equivalents (*Teacher's Edition Vol 1* p. 202B) items having the same value

Spanish Cognates

These words take advantage of what students and their families may know in their home language in order to accelerate the acquisition of math concepts in English.

to convert convertir
liter litro

Review Key Ideas

Have students complete the activity below to make sure that they understand the lesson concept.

Con tus compañeros decide cuál es más fácil, determinar cuántas pulgadas hay en 342 yardas o determinar cuántos centímetros hay en 342 kilómetros. Explica por qué.	Work together to decide which is easier: finding how many inches are in 342 yards or finding how many centimeters are in 342 kilometers. Explain why.

Multiplying by Multiples of 10

Preview Key Ideas

Briefly preview the key ideas of the lesson in the students' primary language so that students can better comprehend the English instruction.

Cuando multiplicas por múltiplos de 10 necesitos poner una cantidad específica de ceros después de el producto.	Multiplying by multiples of 10 involves multiplying facts and then placing a specific number of 0s after the product.

Access Vocabulary

Before or during the lesson, be sure to clarify the words below:

power (*Teacher's Edition Vol 1* p. 204A) the number of times a given number or expression is multiplied by itself

factor (*Teacher's Edition Vol 1* p. 204B) any of the numbers in an algebraic expression that, when multiplied together, form a product

Spanish Cognates

These words take advantage of what students and their families may know in their home language in order to accelerate the acquisition of math concepts in English.

multiple múltiplo
result resultado

Review Key Ideas

Have students complete the activity below to make sure that they understand the lesson concept.

Explica como te ayuda saber 1,000 × 1,000 = 1,000,000 (un millón) cuando tratas de multiplicar rápido 2,000 × 3,000.	Explain how knowing that 1,000 × 1,000 = 1,000,000 (one million) will help you quickly multiply 2,000 by 3,000.

Practice with Multiples of 10

Preview Key Ideas

Briefly preview the key ideas of the lesson in the students' primary language so that students can better comprehend the English instruction.

En esta lección convertirás medidas del sistema métrico. Vas a utilizar hechos métricos y tu conocimiento de la multiplicación para resolver problemas de palabras. Ten cuidado cuando multipliques por los múltiplos de 10. Recuerda contar el número de 0s en dos factores.	In this lesson we will convert measurements within the metric system. We will use metric facts and multiplication skills to solve word problems. We must pay careful attention when we multiply by multiples of 10. Remember to count the number of 0s in the two factors.

Access Vocabulary

Before or during the lesson, be sure to clarify the terms below:

walking stride (*Student Edition* p. 207) the measure of the width between feet when walking
Big Ben (*Student Edition* p. 207) Big Ben is a famous clock in a tower in London, England.

Spanish Cognates

These words take advantage of what students and their families may know in their home language in order to accelerate the acquisition of math concepts in English.

minutes minutos
seconds segundos

Review Key Ideas

Have students complete the activity below to make sure that they understand the lesson concept.

Usando un diagrama Venn, compara el sistema métrico con el sistema Inglés. Muestra que es lo más fácil y que es lo más difícil de cada sistema de unidades.	Using a Venn diagram, compare the metric system with the system of customary units. Show what is easy and what is difficult about each system.

Rounding and Approximating

Preview Key Ideas

Briefly preview the key ideas of the lesson in the students' primary language so that students can better comprehend the English instruction.

En esta lección aprenderás una importante destreza conocido como redondear. Redondear es la idea de utilizar un número para describir cuántos son aproximadamente. Redondear se usa cuando no necesitas un número exacto para tu calculación o cuando necesitas verificar un cálculo.	In this lesson, we will learn an important skill known as rounding. Rounding is the idea of using a number to describe *about* how many. Rounding is useful when we do not need an exact answer to a calculation or when we wish to check a computation.

Access Vocabulary

Before or during the lesson, be sure to clarify the terms below:

swim goggles (*Student Edition* p. 209) airtight glasses used by swimmers to protect their eyes and improve underwater vision
take in (*Student Edition* p. 209) how much money will be collected at a sale

Spanish Cognates

These words take advantage of what students and their families may know in their home language in order to accelerate the acquisition of math concepts in English.

to approximate aproximar
to round redondear

Review Key Ideas

Have students complete the activity below to make sure that they understand the lesson concept.

Con tus compañeros describan una situación donde es más útil aproximar una respuesta que usar cálculos exactos.	Work together to describe a situation where it is more useful to estimate an answer than to use an exact calculation.

Approximating Answers

Preview Key Ideas

Briefly preview the key ideas of the lesson in the students' primary language so that students can better comprehend the English instruction.

En esta lección usarás números para aproximar respuestas a problemas matemáticos. Cuando tú aproximas una respuesta, no tienes que dar solo un número, puedes dar dos y decir que la respuesta está entre esos dos números. Eso se llama límite superior y límite inferior.	In this lesson we will use numbers to approximate answers to math problems. When we approximate an answer, we do not have to give just one number. We can give two numbers and say that the answer is between those two numbers. We call those *upper* and *lower bounds*.

Access Vocabulary

Before or during the lesson, be sure to clarify the terms below:

actual area (*Student Edition* p. 210) true area measurement; The word *actual* is a false Spanish cognate because it is written exactly the same but means something different. In Spanish *actual* means "at the present time."
range (*Teacher's Edition Vol 1* p. 210B) the limits between which something varies

Spanish Cognates

These words take advantage of what students and their families may know in their home language in order to accelerate the acquisition of math concepts in English.

precise preciso
exact exacto

Review Key Ideas

Have students complete the activity below to make sure that they understand the lesson concept.

Con tu grupo, haz una lista de situaciones donde sería muy importante hallar una respuesta precisa en vez de una aproximada.	Brainstorm situations when you would want to find a precise answer rather than an approximate answer.

Practice with Approximating

Preview Key Ideas

Briefly preview the key ideas of the lesson in the students' primary language so that students can better comprehend the English instruction.

En la lección de hoy vas a aproximar las respuestas a problemas de multiplicación con números polidígitos y vas a explorar diferentes métodos para mejorar tu aproximación a un número más preciso.	In today's lesson, we will approximate answers to multidigit multiplication problems and find ways to approximate closer to the actual answer.

Access Vocabulary

Before or during the lesson, be sure to clarify the phrases below:

had her 37th birthday (*Student Edition* p. 216) commemorated her birthday
There is no single best approximation method. (*Teacher's Edition Vol 1* p. 216) Many approximation methods are useful and valuable in different situations.
leap year (*Student Edition* p. 216) a year containing an extra day; Every year whose number is divisible by four is a leap year. In a leap year, there are 366 days instead of 365. The additional day falls on February 29.

Spanish Cognates

These words take advantage of what students and their families may know in their home language in order to accelerate the acquisition of math concepts in English.

exact exacto
to calculate calcular

Review Key Ideas

Have students complete the activity below to make sure that they understand the lesson concept.

Explica los efectos de redondear los factores hacia arriba o hacia abajo para aproximar los productos.	Explain the effects of rounding factors up or down to approximate products.

Multiplication: Two-Digit by One-Digit

Preview Key Ideas

Briefly preview the key ideas of the lesson in the students' primary language so that students can better comprehend the English instruction.

Hoy vas a multiplicar números de dos dígitos por un dígito, y vas a emplear la aproximación para verificar tus respuestas.	Today we will multiply two-digit numbers by one-digit numbers and use approximation to check our answers.

Access Vocabulary

Before or during the lesson, be sure to clarify the terms below:

school fundraiser (*Student Edition* p. 218) an event, sale, or effort organized to gather money for activities at school
flats (*Student Edition* p. 219) large, flat, square trays for storing plants

Spanish Cognates
These words take advantage of what students and their families may know in their home language in order to accelerate the acquisition of math concepts in English.

to align alinear
to explain explicar

Review Key Ideas

Have students complete the activity below to make sure that they understand the lesson concept.

Explica las semejanzas entre multiplicar por un número de dos dígitos y por un número de un dígito. ¿En qué se diferencian?	Explain how the process of multiplying by a two-digit number is similar to and different from multiplying by a one-digit number.

Multiplication: Three-Digit by One-Digit

Preview Key Ideas

Briefly preview the key ideas of the lesson in the students' primary language so that students can better comprehend the English instruction.

Hoy vas a multiplicar números de tres dígitos por un dígito, y vas a emplear la aproximación para verificar tus respuestas.	Today we will multiply three-digit numbers by one-digit numbers and use approximation to check our answers.

Access Vocabulary

Before or during the lesson, be sure to clarify the word and phrase below:

make 72 cents (*Student Edition* p. 222) In this sentence the word *make* means "earn."
altogether (*Student Edition* p. 222) in all; in total

Spanish Cognates

These words take advantage of what students and their families may know in their home language in order to accelerate the acquisition of math concepts in English.

to verify verificar
to correct corregir
multiplicand multiplicando

Review Key Ideas

Have students complete the activity below to make sure that they understand the lesson concept.

Con un compañero o compañera haz una explicación con ilustración del proceso de multiplicar números de un dígito por un número de tres dígitos.	Work in pairs to illustrate an explanation of the process of multiplying a one-digit number by a three-digit number.

Multiplication Review

Preview Key Ideas

Briefly preview the key ideas of the lesson in the students' primary language so that students can better comprehend the English instruction.

Hoy vas a practicar multiplicando números de dos o de tres dígitos por números de un solo dígito.	Today we will practice multiplying two-digit or three-digit numbers by a one-digit number and review approximations of products.

Access Vocabulary

Before or during the lesson, be sure to clarify the words and phrase below:

pay a fine (*Student Edition* p. 224) pay an extra fee for not following the rules
camping (*Student Edition* p. 227) living outdoors for a short period of time as recreation
invest (*Student Edition* p. 224) to put money to use for the purpose of obtaining profit or income

Spanish Cognates

These words take advantage of what students and their families may know in their home language in order to accelerate the acquisition of math concepts in English.

plan plan
service servicio
factor factor

Review Key Ideas

Have students complete the activity below to make sure that they understand the lesson concept.

Describe las maneras más cortas que usas para resolver multiplicaciones de dos dígitos por dos dígitos. Dibuja en un cartel los pasos a seguir, pasa que tus compañeros tengan una idea de cómo lo hiciste.	Describe multiplication shortcuts you use to solve two-digit by two-digit multiplication problems. Draw a step-by-step storyboard for others to follow.

Exponents

Preview Key Ideas

Briefly preview the key ideas of the lesson in the students' primary language so that students can better comprehend the English instruction.

Los exponentes nos dan una manera rápida para indicar cuántas veces se usa un factor.	Exponents provide a short way to indicate the number of times a number is used as a factor.

Access Vocabulary

Before or during the lesson, be sure to clarify the terms below:

recall (*Student Edition* p. 229) remember
dimensions (*Teacher's Edition Vol 1* p. 228B) the measurements of a specific geometric shape
original height (*Teacher's Edition Vol 1* p. 228B) the starting height; the first measurement of height

Spanish Cognates

These words take advantage of what students and their families may know in their home language in order to accelerate the acquisition of math concepts in English.

exponent exponente
base base

Review Key Ideas

Have students complete the activity below to make sure that they understand the lesson concept.

Explica y muestra que quiere decir n^2. Etiqueta la base y el exponente.	Explain and show what n^2 means. Label the base and the exponent.

Perimeter and Area

Preview Key Ideas

Briefly preview the key ideas of the lesson in the students' primary language so that students can better comprehend the English instruction.

En esta lección repasaremos el área y el perímetro. El perímetro es la distancia alrededor de un objeto y el área es el número de unidades al cuadrado que está adentro de el objeto. Usaremos la suma para encontrar el perímetro y la multiplicación para encontrar el área.	In this lesson we will review area and perimeter. Perimeter is the distance around an object, and area is the number of square units that fit inside it. We will use addition to find the perimeter of objects and multiplication to find the area of objects.

Access Vocabulary

Before or during the lesson, be sure to clarify the terms and phrase below:

computing (*Teacher's Edition Vol 1* p. 244–245) finding out or calculating using mathematics
m (*Teacher's Edition Vol 1* p. 244–245) symbol for meter, the fundamental metric length
backyards (*Student Edition* p. 244) the land behind houses belonging to the home owners
one lap of the pool (*Student Edition* p. 245) the length of the pool and back

Spanish Cognates
These words take advantage of what students and their families may know in their home language in order to accelerate the acquisition of math concepts in English.

distance distancia
perimeter perímetro
area área

Review Key Ideas

Have students complete the activity below to make sure that they understand the lesson concept.

Dibuja un jardín y úsalo para explicar el área y el perímetro.	Make a drawing of a garden and use it to explain perimeter and area.

Multiplication: Two-Digit by Two-Digit

Preview Key Ideas

Briefly preview the key ideas of the lesson in the students' primary language so that students can better comprehend the English instruction.

Hoy vamos a aprender un proceso para multiplicar números de dos dígitos. El producto de dos números con dos dígitos puede encontrarse multiplicando los números por partes.	Today we will learn a process for multiplying two digit numbers. The product of two two-digit numbers can be found by thinking of the multiplication in parts.

Access Vocabulary

Before or during the lesson, be sure to clarify the terms below:

shortcut (*Student Edition* p. 249) a way that is shorter than the ordinary way; a way that saves time or effort

makes sense (*Student Edition* p. 248) has reasonable logical; has an understandable meaning

rent each bus (*Student Edition* p. 249) When groups want to take a special trip, they may rent, or charter, a bus. This is different from a school or city bus.

Spanish Cognates

These words take advantage of what students and their families may know in their home language in order to accelerate the acquisition of math concepts in English.

diagram diagrama
fertilize fertilizer

Review Key Ideas

Have students complete the activity below to make sure that they understand the lesson concept.

Completa el organizador Venn para mostrar las semejanzas y diferencias entre la multiplicación de números con un solo dígito y la multiplicación con números polidígitos.	Complete a graphic organizer, such as a Venn diagram, to show the similarities and differences between single-digit and multidigit multiplication.

Applying Multiplication

Preview Key Ideas

Briefly preview the key ideas of the lesson in the students' primary language so that students can better comprehend the English instruction.

En esta lección usaremos la multiplicación para resolver problemas en situaciones reales, así cómo; comprando cosas de una tienda, sacando medidas ó pesando.	In this lesson we will use multiplication to solve problems in real-life situations, such as buying things from a store, measuring, and weighing.

Access Vocabulary

Before or during the lesson, be sure to clarify the words below:

CD (*Student Edition* p. 250) compact disc
recycling (*Student Edition* p. 252) collecting and preparing resources to be used again
drugstore (*Student Edition* p. 252) pharmacy; a store that sells medicine and prepares prescription drugs ordered by a doctor
profit (*Teacher's Edition Vol 1* p. 250B) the amount earned from sales minus the cost of the items

Spanish Cognates

These words take advantage of what students and their families may know in their home language in order to accelerate the acquisition of math concepts in English.

factor factor
product producto
combination combinación

Review Key Ideas

Have students complete the activity below to make sure that they understand the lesson concept. Have students work in pairs. The **Four Cube Multiplication Game** is located in the *Student Edition* on page 253.

Con tu compañero(a), juega el Four Cube Multiplication Game. *Expliquen las estrategias que usaron para jugar el juego.*	Play the **Four Cube Multiplication Game** with a partner. Discuss and explain your strategies for playing the game.

Multiplication Practice

Preview Key Ideas

Briefly preview the key ideas of the lesson in the students' primary language so that students can better comprehend the English instruction.

Hoy practicamos la multiplicación de números de dos dígitos. Recuerda siempre empezar a multiplicar los dígitos en la posición de valor de unidades.	Today we will practice multiplication of two-digit numbers. Remember to start by multiplying the digits in the ones place first.

Access Vocabulary

Before or during the lesson, be sure to clarify the terms and phrase below:

ice-cube maker (*Student Edition* p. 254) a machine in the freezer compartment of a refrigerator that automatically fills with water and makes ice cubes
magazine subscriptions (*Student Edition* p. 254) payments for magazines usually delivered through the mail
trampoline (*Student Edition* p. 254) an elastic device on which a person jumps in order to bounce and jump high
so far off (*Student Edition* p. 255) not possible; impossible
square footage (*Student Edition* p. 254) total amount based on measurement in feet
raise (*Student Edition* p. 254) collect money for a certain cause

Spanish Cognates

These words take advantage of what students and their families may know in their home language in order to accelerate the acquisition of math concepts in English.

approximation aproximación
methods métodos

Review Key Ideas

Have students complete the activity below to make sure that they understand the lesson concept.

Escriba una descripción e incluye una ilustración de un ejemplo de cuando sería mejor hallar una respuesta exacta y otro de cuando sería mejor aproximar una respuesta.	Write a description, and include an illustration of an example of when it is better to find an exact answer and another example of when it is better to find an approximate answer.

Multiplication: Three-Digit by Two-Digit

Preview Key Ideas

Briefly preview the key ideas of the lesson in the students' primary language so that students can better comprehend the English instruction.

En esta lección aprenderemos un algoritmo para multiplicar números de tres dígitos por números de dos dígitos. Este proceso es similar al de multiplicar números de dos dígitos por números de dos dígitos.	In this lesson we will learn an algorithm for multiplying three-digit numbers by two-digit numbers. Multiplying a three-digit number by a two-digit number is similar to multiplying a two-digit number by a two-digit number.

Access Vocabulary

Before or during the lesson, be sure to clarify the words and phrase below:

points (*Student Edition* p. 258) The term *points* was previously introduced with the definition of "specific places on a graph." In this example, *points* means "the units of scoring in a game."
fit (*Student Edition* p. 259) apply to; match
trial and error (*Student Edition* p. 258) the practice of trying one thing after another until the desired result is achieved
bleachers (*Student Edition* p. 258) bench seats tiered for an audience
pep rally (*Student Edition* p. 258) an assembly of students gathered to cheer for a sports team

Spanish Cognates

These words take advantage of what students and their families may know in their home language in order to accelerate the acquisition of math concepts in English.

digit dígito
instruction instrucción
error error

Review Key Ideas

Have students complete the activity below to make sure that they understand the lesson concept. Have students work in pairs.

Con tu compañero(a) escribe e ilustra un problema narrativo empleando números de tres dígitos multiplicados por números de dos dígitos para que tus compañeros lo resuelvan.	Write and illustrate a story problem using multiplication of a three-digit number by a two-digit number for others to solve.

Converting Customary Units

Preview Key Ideas

If students have lived outside the United States, they may be much more familiar with the metric system. These students may need extra help to learn the customary units of measure. Briefly preview the key ideas of the lesson in the students' primary language so that students can better comprehend the English instruction.

En esta lección vas a convertir diferentes medidas usando el sistema Inglés. También practicaremos a aproximar medidas y solucionar problemas narrativos empleando el sistema inglés.	In this lesson, we are going to convert between customary units of measurement, practice estimating measures, and solve problems using customary units of measure.

Access Vocabulary

Before or during the lesson, be sure to clarify the words below:

plaid (*Student Edition* p. 267) a pattern of stripes at right angles
matches (*Teacher's Edition Vol 1* p. 264B) items that are exactly equal to or like another
converting (*Teacher's Edition Vol 1* p. 264B) changing one thing into another thing; exchanging for an equivalent

Spanish Cognates

These words take advantage of what students and their families may know in their home language in order to accelerate the acquisition of math concepts in English.

volume volumen
units unidades

Review Key Ideas

Have students complete the activity below to make sure that they understand the lesson concept.

Haz un dibujo o cartel con representaciones típicas de las medidas del sistema Inglés. Por ejemplo, la leche se vende por galones. Dibuja un galón de leche.	Draw or make a poster with representations of typical items in customary units of measure. For example, milk is sold in gallons; draw a gallon of milk.

Application of Multiplication

Preview Key Ideas

Briefly preview the key ideas of the lesson in the students' primary language so that students can better comprehend the English instruction.

En esta lección practicaremos a aproximar respuestas y a multiplicar números polidígitos. También, aprenderemos cuando debemos usar la multiplicación para resolver varias situaciones.	In this lesson, we will practice approximating answers and multiplying multidigit numbers. We will learn when to use multiplication in a variety of situations.

Access Vocabulary

Before or during the lesson, be sure to clarify the words below:

advertising space (*Student Edition* p. 270) area set aside to advertise in a magazine or newspaper
rolls (*Teacher's Edition Vol 1* p. 268B) to move by throwing something forward making it turn over and over
yield (*Student Edition* p. 271) return or give back
spend (*Student Edition* p. 268) the amount of time used to do something

Spanish Cognates

These words take advantage of what students and their families may know in their home language in order to accelerate the acquisition of math concepts in English.

correct correcto
to multiply multiplicar

Review Key Ideas

Have students complete the activity below to make sure that they understand the lesson concept.

Haz una tabla que contenga todas las medidas del sistema Inglés. Incluye pulgadas, pies, yardas y millas.	Make an equivalency chart of the customary units of measurement. Include inches, feet, yards, and miles.

Multiplying Multidigit Numbers

Preview Key Ideas

Briefly preview the key ideas of the lesson in the students' primary language so that students can better comprehend the English instruction.

En esta lección vamos a aprender a multiplicar grandes números polidígitos. También aprenderemos a notar errores en computaciones. Esta nos ayuda a corregir nuestro trabajo.	In this lesson we are going to learn to multiply greater multidigit numbers. We will also learn to spot errors in computation. This helps us correct our own work.

Access Vocabulary

Before or during the lesson, be sure to clarify the words below:

process (*Teacher's Edition Vol 1* p. 272B) the series of operations performed in doing a math problem
spot (*Teacher's Edition Vol 1* p. 272B) to see or find
errors (*Teacher's Edition Vol 1* p. 272B) mistakes

Spanish Cognates

These words take advantage of what students and their families may know in their home language in order to accelerate the acquisition of math concepts in English.

partial product producto parcial
adequate adecuado

Review Key Ideas

Have students complete the activity below to make sure that they understand the lesson concept.

Haz una lista de profesiones que usen la multiplicación de números polidígitos. Así como; carpinteros, contadores, conductor de camiones y así sucesivamente.	Brainstorm a list of careers that use multidigit multiplication, such as carpenters, accountants, truck drivers, and so on.

Using Multiplication

Preview Key Ideas

Briefly preview the key ideas of the lesson in the students' primary language so that students can better comprehend the English instruction.

Hoy multiplicaremos usando grandes números polidígitos. Recuerda que la multiplicación puede ser usada en varias situaciones.	Today we will multiply using greater multidigit numbers. Multiplication can be used in a variety of situations.

Access Vocabulary

Before or during the lesson, be sure to clarify the terms below:

relation signs (*Student Edition* p. 277) symbols that show the connection between two numbers
falls within (*Teacher's Edition Vol 1* p. 276B) can be found between the lowest number and the highest number

Spanish Cognates

These words take advantage of what students and their families may know in their home language in order to accelerate the acquisition of math concepts in English.

cost costo
relation relación

Review Key Ideas

Have students complete the activity below to make sure that they understand the lesson concept. Have students work in pairs. The **More or Less Game** is located in the *Student Edition* on page 277.

Con tu compañero(a), discutan como se le explicaría las reglas del More or Less Game *a un miembro de tu familia.*	Play the **More or Less Game** with a partner and discuss how you would explain the rules of the game to a family member.

Approximating Products

Preview Key Ideas

Briefly preview the key ideas of the lesson in the students' primary language so that students can better comprehend the English instruction.

Hoy solucionamos problemas que faltan unos dígitos. Usamos las claves, tal cómo posición de valor del número que vemos para decirnos cuán grande es el número.	Today we will solve problems involving missing digits. We will use clues, such as the place value of the number that we can see, to tell us how big the number is.

Access Vocabulary

Before or during the lesson, be sure to clarify the terms below:

rationales (*Teacher's Edition Vol 1* p. 278B) a reasonable or logical explanation
double-check the answer (*Teacher's Edition Vol 1* p. 278B) look over work, then check it again for errors
supply room (*Student Edition* p. 279) storage place for materials
each case (*Student Edition* p. 278) every example or exercise

Spanish Cognates

These words take advantage of what students and their families may know in their home language in order to accelerate the acquisition of math concepts in English.

approximation aproximación
rationale racional

Review Key Ideas

Have students complete the activity below to make sure that they understand the lesson concept.

Selecciona un problema narrativo de la lección. Subraya las claves en el problema y haz una nube arriba del problema explicando cómo estas claves te dicen una parte de la respuesta.	Select one problem from the book. Underline the clues in the problem and create speech bubbles to explain how this clue tells you a part of the answer.

Learning about Percentages

Preview Key Ideas

Briefly preview key ideas of the lesson in the students' primary language so that students can better comprehend the English instruction.

Porciento *significa una "cantidad de 100." Los porcentajes son usados en muchas ocaciones en nuestra vida diaria. En esta lección miraremos fotos de tazas de medidas llenas de líquido y estimaremos el porciento de líquido en cada taza de medidas.*	*Percent* means "out of 100." Percentages are used in many situations in our daily lives. In this lesson we will look at pictures of beakers filled with liquid and estimate the percent full of each beaker.

Access Vocabulary

Before or during the lesson, be sure to clarify the terms and phrase below:

beaker (*Student Edition* p. 294) a special glass container with standard measurements noted on the side that is used in laboratory experiments with liquid
halving (*Teacher's Edition Vol 2* p. 294B) dividing into two equal parts
standard percents (*Student Edition* p. 294) common percentages that are easily recognized, such as 100%, 75%, 50%, and 25%
true or false (*Student Edition* p. 295) a common way of posing test questions

Spanish Cognates

These words take advantage of what students and their families may know in their home language in order to accelerate the acquisition of math concepts in English.

false falso
situations situaciones

Review Key Ideas

Have students complete the activity below to make sure that they understand the lesson concept. Have students work in pairs.

Explica la palabra porcentaje. Usa ejemplos de la vida real para respaldar tu definición.	Explain the word *percent*. Use real-life examples to support your definition.

Percent Benchmarks

Preview Key Ideas

Briefly preview key ideas of the lesson in the students' primary language so that students can better comprehend the English instruction.

En esta lección estimaremos porcentajes y medidas para encontrar montos exactos. Usaremos porcentajes estándar, o puntos de referencia, para encontrar la altura de los líquidos en las tazas. La mitad de algo y 50 porciento de algo es lo mismo.	In this lesson we will estimate percentages and measure to find exact amounts. We will use standard percentages, or benchmarks, to find the height of liquids in beakers. Half of something and 50 percent of something are the same. One quarter of something and 25 percent of something are the same.

Access Vocabulary

Before or during the lesson, be sure to clarify the terms below:

cm (*Student Edition* p. 296) the symbol for the word *centimeter*
quarter (*Student Edition* p. 296) 25% or $\frac{1}{4}$ of something

Spanish Cognates

These words take advantage of what students and their families may know in their home language in order to accelerate the acquisition of math concepts in English.

fraction fracción
equivalent equivalente

Review Key Ideas

Have students complete the activity below to make sure that they understand the lesson concept. Have students work in groups of four.

Da una fracción equivalente para cada porcentaje de abajo o un porcentaje equivalente para cada fracción. Selecciona un ejemplo y explícalo con tus propias palabras. *50% de 1 =* *$12\frac{1}{2}$% de 1 =* *$\frac{3}{4}$ de 1 =* *$\frac{1}{4}$ de 1 =*	Give an equivalent fraction for each percentage below or an equivalent percentage for each fraction below: Select one example and explain it in your own words. 50% of 1 = $12\frac{1}{2}$% of 1 = $\frac{3}{4}$ of 1 = $\frac{1}{4}$ of 1 =

Understanding $12\frac{1}{2}\%$ and $\frac{1}{8}$

Preview Key Ideas

Briefly preview key ideas of the lesson in the students' primary language so that students can better comprehend the English instruction.

En esta lección practicaremos a hallar porcentajes y fracciones de números enteros. Un octavo de algo y $12\frac{1}{2}\%$ de algo significan lo mismo.	In this lesson we will practice finding percentages and fractions of whole numbers. One eighth of something and $12\frac{1}{2}\%$ of something are the same.

Access Vocabulary

Before or during the lesson, be sure to clarify the words and phrases below:

crafts (*Student Edition* p. 299) items made by an individual rather than made by machines or in a factory
run a booth at the craft fair (*Student Edition* p. 299) to set up a table at a fair to display and sell crafts
up front (*Student Edition* p. 299) get paid before any work is done or profit is known
crease (*Teacher's Edition Vol 2* p. 298B) a mark or line made by folding

Spanish Cognates

These words take advantage of what students and their families may know in their home language in order to accelerate the acquisition of math concepts in English.

standard estándar
logic lógica
segmented segmentado

Review Key Ideas

Have students complete the activity below to make sure that they understand the lesson concept.

Explica como $\frac{1}{8}$ de un objeto es más pequeño que $\frac{1}{4}$. Puedes dibujar o construir un modelo para mostrar el concepto.	Using labels and drawings, demonstrate and explain how $\frac{1}{8}$ of an object is smaller than $\frac{1}{4}$ of the same object.

Applying Percent Benchmarks

Preview Key Ideas

Briefly preview key ideas of the lesson in the students' primary language so that students can better comprehend the English instruction.

En esta lección usaremos porcentajes en relación con medidas. Cuando sabemos el 50 porciento de la longitud de algo, nosotros podemos encontrar toda la longitud del mismo. Lo mismo sería cuando queremos saber otros porcentajes.	In this lesson we will use percentages in relation to measurements. We can find the whole length if we know the measurement that equals 50 percent of a length. The same is true for other percentages.

Access Vocabulary

Before or during the lesson, be sure to clarify the words below:

clue (*Student Edition* p. 303) information or indication that can help a person solve a question, puzzle, or problem
proportion (*Teacher's Edition Vol 2* p. 302–303) the relation of one thing to another with respect to size, number, or amount; ratio
mystery (*Student Edition* p. 303) something that is not known

Spanish Cognates
These words take advantage of what students and their families may know in their home language in order to accelerate the acquisition of math concepts in English.

percentage porcentaje
mystery misterio
solution solución

Review Key Ideas

Have students complete the activity below to make sure that they understand the lesson concept.

Examina bien los carteles que muestran las familias de hilo. Explica por qué será que los hilos que muestran 25% son todos de diferentes longitudes. Explica cómo el mismo porcentaje (25%) puede representar diferentes longitudes.	Use pictures and labels to explain how the 25%-string lengths on the string family posters are different. Explain how the same percentage (25%) could represent different lengths.

Decimals and Stopwatches

Preview Key Ideas

Briefly preview key ideas of the lesson in the students' primary language so that students can better comprehend the English instruction.

En esta lección aprenderemos a leer decimales en un cronómetro y a convertir decimales a fracciones y porcentajes. La palabra cent *viene de una palabra Latina que significa "cien". Un cronómetro común mostrará minutos, segundos y centésimas de segundos.*	In this lesson we will learn to read decimals on a stopwatch and convert decimals to fractions and percentages. The word *cent* comes from a Latin word meaning "hundred." A common stopwatch display will show minutes, seconds, and hundredths of seconds.

Access Vocabulary

Before or during the lesson, be sure to clarify the words and phrase below:

stopwatch (*Student Edition* p. 308) a special watch designed to measure rapid speeds or short intervals of time; The Spanish word for stopwatch is *cronómetro. Crono* means "time" and *metro* means "measure."
cycle (*Teacher's Edition Vol 2* p. 308B) to make a complete round
Snap your fingers. (*Student Edition* p. 308) make a quick popping sound by quickly rubbing the thumb and middle finger together

Spanish Cognates

These words take advantage of what students and their families may know in their home language in order to accelerate the acquisition of math concepts in English.

centiseconds centisegundos
decimal decimal

Review Key Ideas

Have students complete the activity below to make sure that they understand the lesson concept.

Ezplica por qué 15.4 es un número mayor que 5.37.	Explain why 15.4 is a greater number than 5.37.

Adding and Subtracting Decimal Numbers

Preview Key Ideas

Briefly preview key ideas of the lesson in the students' primary language so that students can better comprehend the English instruction.

En esta lección sumaremos y sustraeremos números decimales. Sumar y sustraer números decimales es como sumar y sustraer números enteros.	In this lesson we will add and subtract decimal numbers. Adding and subtracting decimal numbers is like adding and subtracting whole numbers of anything.

Access Vocabulary

Before or during the lesson, be sure to clarify the words and phrase below:

as quickly as they could (*Teacher's Edition Vol 2* p. 310B) a phrase used to describe the way someone tried to complete a task with speed
challenge *(Student Edition* p. 310) competition
descending (*Teacher's Edition Vol 2* p. 310–311) moving from a higher number or place to a lower number or place

Spanish Cognates

These words take advantage of what students and their families may know in their home language in order to accelerate the acquisition of math concepts in English.

percent porciento
fraction fracción
descend descienda

Review Key Ideas

Have students complete the activity below to make sure that they understand the lesson concept. Have students work in pairs. The **Greater Number Card Game** is located in the *Student Edition* on page 311.

Con tu compañero(a) juega el **Greater Number Card Game**. *Discute y explica el método que utilizas para encontrar el número mayor.*	Play the **Greater Number Card Game** with a partner. Discuss and explain your method for finding the greater number.

Number Lines

Preview Key Ideas

Briefly preview key ideas of the lesson in the students' primary language so that students can better comprehend the English instruction.

En esta lección aprenderemos cuándo y cómo poner fracciones, decimales y porcentajes de 1 en líneas numeradas. Una línea numerada esta dividida por segmentos iguales y cada marca significa una distancia.	In this lesson we will learn how and where to put fractions, decimals, and percentages of 1 on number lines. A number line is divided into equal segments. Each mark stands for a distance.

Access Vocabulary

Before or during the lesson, be sure to clarify the terms below:

centisecond (*Student Edition* p. 312) hundredth of a second
target decimal (*Student Edition* p. 312) the time at which you should try to stop your stopwatch
bar (*Student Edition* p. 313) the straight, horizontal line being measured in Lesson 7.7

Spanish Cognates

These words take advantage of what students and their families may know in their home language in order to accelerate the acquisition of math concepts in English.

total total
difference diferencia

Review Key Ideas

Have students complete the activity below to make sure that they understand the lesson concept. Distribute colored pencils or markers.

Haz una línea numerada dividida por diez segmentos. Marca 10 porciento, 50 porciento y 25 porciento. Usa un color diferente para cada porcentajes.	Make a number line divided into ten segments. Mark 10 percent, 50 percent, and 25 percent. Use a different color for each percentage.

Understanding 10% and $\frac{1}{10}$

Preview Key Ideas

Briefly preview key ideas of the lesson in the students' primary language so that students can better comprehend the English instruction.

En esta lección aprenderás que el 10 porciento de una cantidad es lo mismo que $\frac{1}{10}$ de para encontrar cualquier porcentaje que sea múltiplo de 10 porciento.	In this lesson we will learn that 10 percent of a quantity is the same as $\frac{1}{10}$ of the same quantity. We will build on what you have learned to find any percentage that is a multiple of 10 percent.

Access Vocabulary

Before or during the lesson, be sure to clarify the terms below:

10%, $\frac{1}{10}$ (*Student Edition* p. 314) different ways to write and say the same fact
same as (*Student Edition* p. 314) equals
portable DVD player (*Student Edition* p. 314) an easily-carried machine used for playing video and/or music

Spanish Cognates

These words take advantage of what students and their families may know in their home language in order to accelerate the acquisition of math concepts in English.

segments segmentos
method método

Review Key Ideas

Have students complete the activity below to make sure that they understand the lesson concept. Have students work in small groups.

Discute la regla que se utiliza para encontrar $\frac{1}{10}$ (o 10 porciento) de un número que es múltiplo de 10. Discute la razón de por qué el atajo sólo funcionará cuando usemos 10 porciento.	Discuss the rule for finding $\frac{1}{10}$ (or 10 percent) of a number that is a multiple of 10. Discuss the reason the shortcut will only work for 10 percent.

Writing Appropriate Fractions

Preview Key Ideas

Briefly preview key ideas of the lesson in the students' primary language so that students can better comprehend the English instruction.

Usaremos fracciones para describir las partes de los números enteros y conjunto de números. El denominador, o el número que se encuentra abajo de la fracción, nos indica cuántas partes iguales hay en un número entero o en el conjunto de números. El numerador, o el número de arriba de una fracción nos indica cuántas de esas partes se deben tomar.	In this lesson we will use fractions to describe parts of wholes and parts of sets. The denominator, or bottom number of a fraction, tells how many equal-sized parts there are in the whole or set. The numerator, or top number of a fraction, describes how many of the equal-sized parts we are dealing with.

Access Vocabulary

Before or during the lesson, be sure to clarify the terms below:

shaded (*Student Edition* p. 330) colored or darkened to distinguish it from the rest of the shape
reasonable (*Teacher's Edition Vol 2* p. 330B) showing or using good sense; sensible
unreasonable (*Teacher's Edition Vol 2* p. 330B) not showing good judgment or sense
set (*Teacher's Edition Vol 2* p. 330B) group
birthday cake (*Student Edition* p. 331) a cake eaten at a birthday celebration that usually has decorative icing and candles
spinner (*Student Edition* p. 331) flat circle divided into sections with a free moving hand that players in a game spin rapidly

Spanish Cognates

These words take advantage of what students and their families may know in their home language in order to accelerate the acquisition of math concepts in English.

numerator numerador
denominator denominador
reasonable razonable
unreasonable irrazonable

Review Key Ideas

Have students complete the activity below to make sure that they understand the lesson concept. Have students work in pairs.

Dibuja muchas líneas, luego sombrea una línea segmentada en cada una. Escribe una fracción abajo de cada línea segmentada. Haz que tu compañero(a) te diga si la fracción que escribiste es razonable o irrazonable y por qué.	Draw several lines. Then shade a line segment on each one. Write a fraction below each line segment. Have your partner tell if the fraction is reasonable or unreasonable and why.

Fractions of Fractions

Preview Key Ideas

Briefly preview key ideas of the lesson in the students' primary language so that students can better comprehend the English instruction.

En esta lección vamos a considerar cómo encontrar una fracción de una fracción. También vamos a ver por qué es natural decir que tomar una fracción de una fracción es multiplicar fracciones. Se puede encontrar la fracción de una fracción de algo multiplicando numeradores y denominadores. El nuevo numerador será el producto de los numeradores. El nuevo denominador será el producto de los denominadores.	In this lesson, we will learn how to find a fraction of a fraction. Taking a fraction of a fraction is called *multiplication of fractions*. A fraction of a fraction can be found by multiplying the numerators and the denominators. The new numerator will be the product of the original numerators. The new denominator will be the product of the original denominators.

Access Vocabulary

Before or during the lesson, be sure to clarify the terms below:

"of" operation (*Student Edition* p. 332A) Some students might refer to multiplication of fractions as finding the fraction "of" a fraction.
submarine sandwich (*Teacher's Edition Vol 2* p. 332–333) a hero; a sandwich made of a small loaf of bread filled with meat, cheese, and vegetables

Spanish Cognates

These words take advantage of what students and their families may know in their home language in order to accelerate the acquisition of math concepts in English.

fraction fracción
product producto

Review Key Ideas

Have students complete the activity below to make sure that they understand the lesson concept. Have students work in small groups.

Con tus compañeros describe e ilustra una regla general para encontrar una fracción de una fracción. ¿Por qué se puede decir que buscar una fracción de una fracción es multiplicar las fracciones?	Describe and illustrate the general rule for finding a fraction of a fraction. Describe why finding a fraction of a fraction is called *multiplication of fractions*.

Fractions and Rational Numbers

Preview Key Ideas

Briefly preview key ideas of the lesson in the students' primary language so that students can better comprehend the English instruction.

En esta lección aprenderemos cómo las fracciones pueden ser representadas con puntos en una línea numerada. Las posiciones en una línea numerada representan los números racionales, los cuales pueden ser escritos cómo fracciones usando cualquier combinación de números, mientras que los denominadores no sean 0.	In this lesson we will learn how fractions can be represented as points on a number line. Positions on a number line represent numbers called *rational numbers*, which can be written like fractions using any combination of numbers, as long as the denominators are not 0.

Access Vocabulary

Before or during the lesson, be sure to clarify the words below:

places (*Teacher's Edition Vol 2* p. 334–335) place value
imagine (*Student Edition* p. 334) picture something in the mind
terminating (*Teacher's Edition Vol 2* p. 334A) coming to a stop or an end

Spanish Cognates

These words take advantage of what students and their families may know in their home language in order to accelerate the acquisition of math concepts in English.

centimeter centímetro
divide dividir
rational numbers números racionales
equivalent equivalente
decimal decimal

Review Key Ideas

Have students complete the activity below to make sure that they understand the lesson concept. Have students work in pairs.

Explícale a tu compañero(a) cómo encontrar los decimales equivalentes de las fracciones. Usa $\frac{2}{5}$ ó $\frac{1}{2}$ para demostrarle el proceso.	Explain to your partner how to find decimal equivalents of fractions. Use $\frac{2}{5}$ or $\frac{1}{2}$ to demonstrate your process.

Probability

Preview Key Ideas

Briefly preview key ideas of the lesson in the students' primary language so that students can better comprehend the English instruction.

En esta lección usaremos fracciones para calcular probabilidades. Las fracciones pueden ayudarnos a pensar acerca de qué tan probable algo pueda ocurrir. Una probabilidad te indica la fracción del tiempo en el cuál un suceso ocurrirá. Por ejemplo, la probabilidad de que una moneda lanzada al aire caiga en cara es 1 de 2 veces ó $\frac{1}{2}$.	In this lesson we will use fractions to calculate probability. Fractions can help us think about how likely it is that something will occur. A probability tells us the fraction of the time in which something is expected to happen. For example, if we flip a coin, it can land on one of its two faces. The probability that the coin will land heads up is 1 result out of 2 equally possible outcomes, or $\frac{1}{2}$.

Access Vocabulary

Before or during the lesson, be sure to clarify the terms and phrase below:

flip a coin (*Student Edition* p. 336) When trying to break a tie or decide who goes first in a competition or other two part decision, we sometimes flip a coin. The coin is tossed or flipped into the air by a neutral person. One competitor calls either heads or tails. If the coin lands on the side he or she called, that person goes first or has the initial advantage.
faces (*Student Edition* p. 336) flat surfaces; coins have two faces and an edge
heads/tails (*Student Edition* p. 336) every monetary coin has a head and a tail. The head is a portrait of some famous individual in United States history. The tail is a scene from history or the state.

Spanish Cognates

These words take advantage of what students and their families may know in their home language in order to accelerate the acquisition of math concepts in English.

description descripción
probability probabilidad
common común

Review Key Ideas

Have students complete the activity below to make sure that they understand the lesson concept.

Explica y muestra como sería jugar limpio. Discute acerca de si el juego sería justo si un jugador tuviera más oportunidades para ganar.	Explain and show what a fair game would be. Discuss whether the game is fair if one player has more opportunities to win.

Probability Experiments

Preview Key Ideas

Briefly preview key ideas of the lesson in the students' primary language so that students can better comprehend the English instruction.

En esta lección resolveremos problemas que se relacionen con la probabilidad. La probabilidad nos puede dar una idea de que tan frecuente algo puede pasar, pero no puede predecir lo que pasará en cada situación.	In this lesson we will solve problems involving probability. Probability can give an idea of how often something is likely to happen, but does not predict what will happen each time.

Access Vocabulary

Before or during the lesson, be sure to clarify the words and phrase below:

expect (*Student Edition* p. 338) to look ahead to an event or item that is certain or likely
What fraction of the time do you think Jimmy will win? (*Student Edition* p. 338) How often do you think Jimmy will win?
fair (*Student Edition* pp. 338–339) gives an equal chance to win

Spanish Cognates

These words take advantage of what students and their families may know in their home language in order to accelerate the acquisition of math concepts in English.

predict predecir
possible posible
experiments experimentos
interpretation interpretación

Review Key Ideas

Have students complete the activity below to make sure that they understand the lesson concept. Have students work in pairs.

Explícale a tu compañero(a) el concepto de la probabilidad y juntos piensen en por lo menos un ejemplo de donde se usa la probabilidad en nuestras vidas cotidianas.	Explain to a partner the concept of probability, and together come up with at least one example of where you see probability used in your daily lives.

Applying Fractions

Preview Key Ideas

Briefly preview key ideas of the lesson in the students' primary language so that students can better comprehend the English instruction.

En esta lección vamos a aprender a encontrar una fracción de un número, dividiendo el número en partes iguales y tomando algunas de estas partes.	In this lesson we will learn to find a fraction of a number by dividing the number into equal parts and taking some of these parts.

Access Vocabulary

Before or during the lesson, be sure to clarify the terms below:

take place (*Student Edition* p. 340) to happen
chemistry set (*Student Edition* p. 340) a collection of chemicals and tools that an amateur would use to do basic chemistry experiments
outcome (*Teacher's Edition Vol 2* p. 340B) a result or consequence; something that happens because of an earlier action, process, or condition

Spanish Cognates

These words take advantage of what students and their families may know in their home language in order to accelerate the acquisition of math concepts in English.

diverse diverso
apply aplica
divide dividir
equal parts partes iguales

Review Key Ideas

Have students complete the activity below to make sure that they understand the lesson concept.

Discute acerca de las estrategias que usaste en el Anything but 10 Game. Describe cómo y cuándo decidiste dejar de lanzar el cubo.	Discuss the strategies you used in the **Anything but 10 Game.** Describe how you decided when to stop rolling.

Probability and Fractions

Preview Key Ideas

Briefly preview key ideas of the lesson in the students' primary language so that students can better comprehend the English instruction.

Hoy vamos a ver que dos diferentes fracciones pueden describir la misma parte de un número entero. Las fracciones que describen la misma parte de un número entero muestran probabilidades iguales. Podemos resolver problemas que impliquen fracciones y probabilidades.	Today we will see that two different fractions can describe the same part of a whole. Fractions show equal probability when they describe the same part of a whole.

Access Vocabulary

Before or during the lesson, be sure to clarify the words and phrase below:

part of a whole (*English Learner Support Guide* p. 83) part of a whole object or set; part of an entire thing
region (*Student Edition* p. 342) a large portion of an area
involving (*Teacher's Edition Vol 2* p. 342B) including as a necessary part
contiguous (*Teacher's Edition Vol 2* p. 342B) touching; in physical contact

Spanish Cognates

These words take advantage of what students and their families may know in their home language in order to accelerate the acquisition of math concepts in English.

circle círculo
region región
contiguous contiguo

Review Key Ideas

Have students complete the activity below to make sure that they understand the lesson concept. Have students work in pairs.

Explica el significado de la palabra denominador. Haz un modelo con un papel doblado, un dibujo u otros materiales para que demuestres lo que entiendes por la palabra denominador.	Explain what the denominator stands for. Make a model with folded paper, a drawing, or another set of materials to demonstrate your understanding.

Equivalent Fractions

Preview Key Ideas

Briefly preview key ideas of the lesson in the students' primary language so that students can better comprehend the English instruction.

En esta lección vamos a ver que las fracciones equivalentes son las que representan la misma cantidad del mismo entero. Hay muchas maneras de escribir fracciones del mismo valor.	In this lesson we will see that equivalent fractions are fractions that represent the same amount of the same thing. There are many different ways to write fractions of the same value.

Access Vocabulary

Before or during the lesson, be sure to clarify the terms and phrase below:

tiny pieces (*Student Edition* p. 344) very small pieces
make equivalent fractions (*Student Edition* p. 345) Here the word *make* means "calculate or find."
represent (*Teacher's Edition Vol 2* p. 344B) to serve as a symbol, sign, or example of

Spanish Cognates

These words take advantage of what students and their families may know in their home language in order to accelerate the acquisition of math concepts in English.

equivalent equivalente
convert convertir
segment segmento

Review Key Ideas

Have students complete the activity below to make sure that they understand the lesson concept. Have students work in small groups.

Describe e ilustra la regla general para hacer una fracción equivalente. Haz un modelo con un papel doblado, un dibujo u otros materiales para demostrar tu conocimiento.	Describe and illustrate the general rule for making an equivalent fraction. Make a model with folded paper, a drawing, or another set of materials to demonstrate your understanding.

Comparing Fractions

Preview Key Ideas

Briefly preview key ideas of the lesson in the students' primary language so that students can better comprehend the English instruction.

En esta lección usaremos fracciones equivalentes para comparar fracciones con denominadores diferentes. Para poder comparar fracciones que tengan diferentes denominadores, es muy útil cambiar el denomidador de cada fracción para que ambas tengan el mismo denominador. Un denominador que frecuentemente funciona, es el resultado del producto de los dos denominadores.	In this lesson we will use equivalent fractions to compare fractions with unlike denominators. To compare fractions that have different denominators, it is helpful to change both of the fractions so they have the same denominator. A new denominator that often works well is the product of the two original denominators.

Access Vocabulary

Before or during the lesson, be sure to clarify the terms below:

field trip (*Student Edition* p. 347) an educational class trip away from school
yards (*Student Edition* p. 347) area of ground next to or surrounding houses or other buildings
mowed (*Student Edition* p. 347) cut grass with a machine

Spanish Cognates

These words take advantage of what students and their families may know in their home language in order to accelerate the acquisition of math concepts in English.

equivalent equivalente
students estudiantes

Review Key Ideas

Have students complete the activity below to make sure that they understand the lesson concept.

Comparte con tus compañeros las maneras que usas para recordar cuál dirección apunta el signo de desigualdad, así como el ejemplo del cocodrillo apuntando con la parte más ancha de la mandíbula hacia el número mayor.	Come up with ways you can remember which direction the inequality sign reads, such as the alligator example, with the widest part of the "jaws" pointing toward the greater number.

Fractions Greater than 1

Preview Key Ideas

Briefly preview key ideas of the lesson in the students' primary language so that students can better comprehend the English instruction.

Hay dos maneras diferentes de escribir fracciones mayores que 1, también llamado números racionales mayores que 1. Una de las maneras es escribiendo un número entero más una fracción menos que uno. Esto algunas veces se llama número mixto. Otra manera sería escribiendo una fracción con un numerador mayor que su denominador. Esto se llama fracción impropia. Desde que los números mixtos y las fracciones impropias pueden ser usadas para representar la misma cantidad, podemos escribir una u otra cuando lo necesitemos.	There are two different ways to write fractions greater than 1, also called *rational numbers greater than 1*. One way is to write a whole number plus a fraction less than one. This is sometimes called a *mixed number*. Another way is to write a fraction with a numerator greater than its denominator. This is called an improper fraction. Since mixed numbers and improper fractions can both be used to represent the same amount, we can write one or the other when needed.

Access Vocabulary

Before or during the lesson, be sure to clarify the terms below:

loaves (*Student Edition* p. 352) plural of loaf; a shaped mass of dough baked into bread
can of frozen orange juice (*Teacher's Edition Vol 2* p. 355A) a container of thick frozen fruit juice
cheese wheel (*Student Edition* p. 352) a circular piece of cheese
convenient (*Student Edition* p. 354) within easy reach; matched to one's needs or purposes
leftover (*Student Edition* p. 355) something that remains unused, such as food after a meal; unused or remaining

Spanish Cognates
These words take advantage of what students and their families may know in their home language in order to accelerate the acquisition of math concepts in English.

mixed number número mixto
improper fraction fracción impropia
units unidades
guitar guitarra

Review Key Ideas

Have students complete the activity below to make sure that they understand the lesson concept.

Haz una explicación de una fracción impropia y un número mixto y por qué es importante tener las dos maneras para expresar las fracciones. Ilustra tus ejemplos.	Create an illustration for an improper fraction or a mixed number and explain why it is helpful to have these two ways to show fractions.

Representing Fractions Greater than 1

Preview Key Ideas

Briefly preview key ideas of the lesson in the students' primary language so that students can better comprehend the English instruction.

En esta lección repasamos varias maneras para nombrar números racionales mayores que 1: fracciones mayores que 1, fracciones equivalentes mayores que 1 y decimales equivalentes simples. También, vamos a practicar a hallar fracciones equivalentes para fracciones mayores que 1.	In this lesson we will review multiple ways to name rational numbers greater than 1: fractions greater than 1, equivalent fractions greater than 1, percents greater than 1, and simple decimal equivalents. We will also practice finding equivalent fractions for fractions greater than 1.

Access Vocabulary

Before or during the lesson, be sure to clarify the terms below:

savings account (*Student Edition* p. 359) money deposited into a bank and held for the depositor
improper fraction (*Student Edition* p. 356) a fraction whose numerator, or top number, is greater than or equal to its denominator, or bottom number
extend (*Student Edition* p. 358) to made longer or to continue

Spanish Cognates

These words take advantage of what students and their families may know in their home language in order to accelerate the acquisition of math concepts in English.

original original
bank banco
process proceso

Review Key Ideas

Have students complete the activity below to make sure that they understand the lesson concept.

Explica por qué para una persona no tiene sentido decir que está "de acuerdo contigo 110%". Incluye una ilustración con tu explicación.	Explain why it doesn't make sense for someone to "agree with you 110%". Include an illustration with your explanation.

Reading a Ruler

Preview Key Ideas

Briefly preview key ideas of the lesson in the students' primary language so that students can better comprehend the English instruction.

Las fracciones son útiles para describir partes de las unidades de medida. Nosotros repasaremos y practicaremos las unidades de medida del sistema inglés para medir la longitud de algunos objetos. Las medidas que obtengamos pueden ser descritas usando fracciones y números mixtos.	Fractions are useful in describing parts of units of measurement. We will review customary units of length and practice measuring objects using customary units of length. Our measurements can be described using fractions and mixed numbers.

Access Vocabulary

Before or during the lesson, be sure to clarify the word and phrases below:

halfway (*Student Edition* p. 360) middle, between two points
How long? (*Student Edition* p. 361) a question asking for a measurement of length
How wide? (*Student Edition* p. 361) a question asking for a measurement of width

Spanish Cognates

These words take advantage of what students and their families may know in their home language in order to accelerate the acquisition of math concepts in English.

describe describir
units unidades
considered considerar

Review Key Ideas

Have students complete the activity below to make sure that they understand the lesson concept. Have students work in pairs.

Dibuja y etiqueta relaciones equivalentes que existe entre diferentes unidades de medida en el sistema inglés. Por ejemplo, 12 pulgadas = 1 pie. Completa dos tablas, una para la longitud y otra para el peso.	Draw and label equivalent relationships in customary units of measure. For example, 12 inches = 1 foot. Complete two charts, one for length and one for weight.

Adding and Subtracting Measurements

Preview Key Ideas

Briefly preview key ideas of the lesson in the students' primary language so that students can better comprehend the English instruction.

Hoy vamos a practicar a sumar y a sustraer medidas descritas como fracciones simples y números mixtos. Nosotros podemos encontrar la suma de dos medidas fraccionales juntando las puntas de cada longitud para así, obtener el total. También, podemos hallar la diferencia entre dos medidas fraccionales juntando la segunda longitud encima de la primera y sustraendo las medidas.	Today we will practice adding and subtracting measurements described as simple fractions and mixed numbers. We can find the sum of two fractional measurements by laying the two lengths end-to-end and measuring the total length. We can find the difference of two fractional measurements by laying the second length on top of the first length and subtracting the measurements.

Access Vocabulary

Before or during the lesson, be sure to clarify the terms below:

bulletin board (*Student Edition* p. 362) a display area on the wall of a classroom to show student work or to show examples tied to the area of study
sticks out (*Student Edition* p. 362) In this example, a piece of wood is in a hole. The wood is longer than a hole is deep; the wood *sticks out.*
trail mix (*Student Edition* p. 363) a snack made of dried fruit, granola, nuts, and seeds

Spanish Cognates

These words take advantage of what students and their families may know in their home language in order to accelerate the acquisition of math concepts in English.

total total
correct correcto
line línea

Review Key Ideas

Have students complete the activity below to make sure that they understand the lesson concept. Have students work in small groups.

Haz una gráfica de tres columnas que enseñe unas situaciones en la casa, en la escuela y en el recreo donde usaríamos la suma y la resta de fracciones.	Complete a three-column chart that shows or names situations at home, at school, and at play for which we would use addition and subtraction of fractions.

Fractions at Home	Fractions at School	Fractions at Play

Adding and Subtracting Fractions

Preview Key Ideas

Briefly preview key ideas of the lesson in the students' primary language so that students can better comprehend the English instruction.

Para sumar y sustraer fracciones que tengan un denominador común, simplemente sumamos y sustraemos los numeradores. Para sumar fracciones con diferentes denominadores, posiblemente necesitamos convertir una o ambas fracciones a una fracción equivalente para que los denominadores tengan un denominador común.	To add and subtract fractions with the same denominator, we simply add or subtract the numerators. To add or subtract fractions with different denominators, we might need to convert one or both of the fractions to an equivalent fraction so that the denominators will be the same.

Access Vocabulary

Before or during the lesson, be sure to clarify the words and phrase below:

numerator (*Student Edition* p. 364) the top number of a fraction
denominator (*Student Edition* p. 364) the bottom number of a fraction
fractions with like denominators (*Teacher's Edition Vol 2* p. 364B) fractions having the same, or identical, denominators

Spanish Cognates

These words take advantage of what students and their families may know in their home language in order to accelerate the acquisition of math concepts in English.

different diferente
problems problemas
fraction fracción

Review Key Ideas

Have students complete the activity below to make sure that they understand the lesson concept. Have students work in pairs.

Explica por qué no puedes sumar o sustraer fracciones con diferentes denominadores sin convertirlos. Haz un modelo con un papel doblado, un dibujo u otros materiales para demostrar tu conocimiento.	Explain why you cannot add or subtract fractions with different denominators without converting them. Make a model with folded paper, a drawing, or another set of material to demonstrate your understanding.

Adding Fractions Greater than 1

Preview Key Ideas

Briefly preview key ideas of the lesson in the students' primary language so that students can better comprehend the English instruction.

Podemos sumar o sustraer fracciones mayores que 1 de la misma manera que sumamos y sustraemos fracciones menores que uno. Sumaremos números mixtos con denominadores iguales y usaremos fracciones equivalentes para sumar números mixtos con denominadores desiguales.	In this lesson we will learn that we can add or subtract fractions greater than 1 the same way we add and subtract fractions less than one. We will add mixed numbers with like denominators and use equivalent fractions to add mixed numbers with unlike denominators.

Access Vocabulary

Before or during the lesson, be sure to clarify the words below:

icing (*Student Edition* p. 367) also called frosting, this creamy, sweet paste is made with sugar and covers the outside of a cake
suppose (*Teacher's Edition Vol 2* p. 366–367) to imagine; to pretend; to think about
convert (*Teacher's Edition Vol 2* p. 366B) to change into

Spanish Cognates

These words take advantage of what students and their families may know in their home language in order to accelerate the acquisition of math concepts in English.

combine combinar
ingredients ingredientes
convert convertir

Review Key Ideas

Have students complete the activity below to make sure that they understand the lesson concept. Have students work in small groups.

Haz una secuencia ilustrada de los pasos necesarios para sumar dos números mixtos. Luego haz otra secuencia ilustrada de los pasos necesarios para restar fracciones impropias.	Make a story board with four or five panels to show the steps of adding two mixed numbers. Then make a second story board with an example of subtracting improper fractions.

Subtracting Fractions Greater than 1

Preview Key Ideas

Briefly preview key ideas of the lesson in the students' primary language so that students can better comprehend the English instruction.

En esta lección nosotros aprendemos que podemos sustraer fracciones mayores que 1 de la misma manera que sustraemos fracciones menores que 1. Sustraeremos números mixtos con denominadores iguales y usaremos fracciones equivalentes para sustraer números mixtos con denominadores desiguales.	In this lesson we will learn that we can subtract fractions greater than 1 the same way we subtract fractions less than 1. We will subtract mixed numbers with like denominators and use equivalent fractions to subtract mixed numbers with unlike denominators.

Access Vocabulary

Before or during the lesson, be sure to clarify the terms and phrase below:

science fair (*Student Edition* p. 369) an event where projects or experiments in science are displayed around a large room and students explain their work; often competitive
good deal (*Student Edition* p. 369) an inexpensive or a low price
turned their problem into (*Teacher's Edition Vol 2* p. 368B) converted or changed their problem to a different form

Spanish Cognates

These words take advantage of what students and their families may know in their home language in order to accelerate the acquisition of math concepts in English.

science ciencia
plastic plástico
calculation calculación

Review Key Ideas

Have students complete the activity below to make sure that they understand the lesson concept.

Crea e ilustra un diagrama Venn para demostrar que el sustraer fracciones mayores que 1 es similar a o diferente a sustraer fracciones menores que 1.	Create a Venn diagram to illustrate how subtracting fractions greater than 1 is similar to and different from subtracting fractions less than 1.

Parts of a Whole

Preview Key Ideas

Briefly preview the key ideas of the lesson in the students' primary language so that students can better comprehend the English instruction.

Nosotros podemos escribir los números del 0 al 1 en diferentes maneras. En esta lección repasamos los conceptos de decimales y demostraremos la relación que tienen con algunas fracciones.	We can write the numbers between 0 and 1 in different ways. In this lesson we will review the concepts of decimals and demonstrate their relationships to corresponding fractions.

Access Vocabulary

Before or during the lesson, be sure to clarify the terms below:

not fair (*Student Edition* p. 384) someone has more of an advantage
unlimited (*Teacher's Edition Vol 2* p. 384B) without limits or restrictions

Spanish Cognates

These words take advantage of what students and their families may know in their home language in order to accelerate the acquisition of math concepts in English.

decimal point punto decimal
different diferente
unlimited ilimitado
affects afecta

Review Key Ideas

Have students complete the activity below to ensure they understand the lesson concept.

Dibuja un ejemplo de la diferencia entre sumar un cero después de un número entero positivo así como, 5 y añadiendo un cero después del último dígito de un número decimal así como, 0.5. Explica la diferencia.	Work with a partner. Draw an example of the difference between inserting a zero after a positive integer such as 5 and inserting a zero after the last digit of a decimal number such as 0.5. Explain the difference.

Decimals and Fractions

Preview Key Ideas

Briefly preview the key ideas of the lesson in the students' primary language so that students can better comprehend the English instruction.

En esta lección aprenderemos la relación entre décimas, centésimas y milésimas. Practicaremos comparando decimales y usando signos de relación. Pensar en las fracciones equivalentes puede ayudarnos a comparar decimales.	In this lesson we will learn the relationship between tenths, hundredths, and thousandths. We will practice comparing decimals and using relation signs. Thinking about equivalent fractions can help us compare decimals.

Access Vocabulary

Before or during the lesson, be sure to clarify the words below:

quiz (*Student Edition* p. 391) a quick test
worth (*Student Edition* p. 389) the value of something
shade (*Teacher's Edition Vol 2* p. 388B) to mark with darkness
magnitude (*Teacher's Edition Vol 2* p. 388–389) greatness of size or degree

Spanish Cognates

These words take advantage of what students and their families may know in their home language in order to accelerate the acquisition of math concepts in English.

express expresar
compare comparar
part parte
magnitude magnitud

Review Key Ideas

Have students complete the activity below to make sure that they understand the lesson concept. Have students work in pairs. Give each set of students six index cards.

Usa seis fichas. Escribe un signo de relación diferente (<, > ó =) en tres de las fichas y escribe el significado de cada una en las otras tres fichas. Mezcla las fichas y haz que tu compañero(a) las empareje.	Write a different relation sign (<, >, or =) on three index cards, and write the meaning of each sign on three additional index cards. Mix up the cards. Have your partner match them.

Comparing Decimals

Preview Key Ideas

Briefly preview the key ideas of the lesson in the students' primary language so that students can better comprehend the English instruction.

En esta lección compararemos decimales con otros decimales. Los decimales pueden ser descritos como mayor que, menor que o igual a otros decimales.	In this lesson we will compare decimals to other decimals. Decimals can be described as greater than, less than, or equal to other decimals.

Access Vocabulary

Before or during the lesson, be sure to clarify the terms and phrase below:

batting averages (*Teacher's Edition Vol 2* p. 392B) percentage of hits based on the opportunities to hit
value (*Teacher's Edition Vol 2* p. 392A) worth
as few coins as possible (*Student Edition* p. 392) form of comparison describing the smallest number of coins possible

Spanish Cognates

These words take advantage of what students and their families may know in their home language in order to accelerate the acquisition of math concepts in English.

compare comparar
sections secciones
cents centavos
equal igual

Review Key Ideas

Have students complete the activity below to make sure that they understand the lesson concept. Have students work in pairs.

Usando tan pocas monedas como sea posible, muestra éstas cantidades: $0.44, $0.37 y $0.75.	Use coins to show quantities such as $0.44, $0.37, and $0.75. Use as few coins as possible.

Ordering Decimals

Preview Key Ideas

Briefly preview the key ideas of the lesson in the students' primary language so that students can better comprehend the English instruction.

En esta lección ordenaremos los decimales. Para comparar dos decimales, podemos poner un grupo de decimales en orden y poner decimales en una línea numerada. Los decimales que compararemos tienen que tener el mismo número de dígitos a la derecha del punto del decimal.	In this lesson we will order decimals. If we can compare two decimals, we can put a set of decimals in order and place decimals on a number line. Decimals that we compare should have the same number of digits to the right of the decimal point.

Access Vocabulary

Before or during the lesson, be sure to clarify the terms below:

demarcations (*Teacher's Edition Vol 2* p. 394B) the markings of boundaries or limits
ordering (*Student Edition* p. 394) placing things in the right or proper positions
ordinarily (*Student Edition* p. 394) usually; in a usual or normal way
proper (*Student Edition* p. 396) appropriate or correct for a specific purpose
mathematical reasoning (*Student Edition* p. 397) the process of drawing conclusions from mathematical facts

Spanish Cognates

These words take advantage of what students and their families may know in their home language in order to accelerate the acquisition of math concepts in English.

in order en orden
list lista
demarcation demarcación

Review Key Ideas

Have students complete the activity below to make sure that they understand the lesson concept. Have students work in pairs.

Juega el **Roll a Decimal Game** *para mostrar tu entendimiento del valor de posición y el comparar números decimales.*	Play the **Roll a Decimal Game** a few times to show your understanding of place value and comparing decimal numbers.

Rounding Decimals

Preview Key Ideas

Briefly preview the key ideas of the lesson in the students' primary language so that students can better comprehend the English instruction.

En esta lección redondearemos decimales. Podemos redondear decimales de la misma manera que redondeamos números enteros, mirando el dígito que se encuentra a la derecha del número que estámos redondeando. En algunas situaciones tenemos que usar nuestro criterio para decidir la mejor manera de redondear números.	In this lesson we will round decimals. We can round decimals the same way we round whole numbers—by looking at the digit to the right of the place in which we are rounding. In real-world situations, we must use our judgment to decide the best way to round numbers.

Access Vocabulary

Before or during the lesson, be sure to clarify the terms and phrase below:

judgment/judgment call (*Teacher's Edition Vol 2* p. 398B) an opinion or decision made by considering the facts
splitting a dinner bill (*Teacher's Edition Vol 2* p. 398B) sharing or dividing the total cost of a dinner by the number of people at the table; *splitting* refers to dividing the cost
conference (*Student Edition* p. 399) meeting

Spanish Cognates

These words take advantage of what students and their families may know in their home language in order to accelerate the acquisition of math concepts in English.

direction dirección
situations situación
digits dígitos

Review Key Ideas

Have students complete the activity below to make sure that they understand the lesson concept. Have students work in small groups.

Con tus compañeros haz un diagrama ilustrado que muestre cómo decidir cuando sería mejor redondear para arriba y cuando para abajo. Discute alguna situación en donde no necesites redondear.	Create an illustrated chart that shows how to decide when to round up and when to round down. Discuss any situations in which you should not round.

Multiplying and Dividing by Powers of 10

Preview Key Ideas

Briefly preview the key ideas of the lesson in the students' primary language so that students can better comprehend the English instruction.

En esta lección vamos a ver que, debido al hecho que las posiciones de valor están basadas en 10, se puede multiplicar o dividir un número por una potencia de 10 simplemente moviendo el punto decimal.	In this lesson we will see that because place values are based on 10, we can multiply or divide a number by a power of 10 simply by moving the decimal point.

Access Vocabulary

Before or during the lesson, be sure to clarify the words below:

quotient (*Teacher's Edition Vol 2* p. 403A) a number or algebraic expression obtained by dividing one number or algebraic expression by another
noisemaker (*Teacher's Edition Vol 2* p. 400B) a device used to make noise at a party or celebration
allowance (*Student Edition* p. 401) a small amount of money given each week to children in some families

Spanish Cognates

These words take advantage of what students and their families may know in their home language in order to accelerate the acquisition of math concepts in English.

value valor
costs costos
direction dirección

Review Key Ideas

Have students complete the activity below to make sure that they understand the lesson concept. Have students work in pairs.

Escoge y escribe una regla para trabajar con decimales e ilústrala también. No te olvides que aunque no este escrito, siempre hay un punto decimal después de la posición de valor de las unidades.	Select and write out one rule of working with decimal points and illustrate that rule. Remember that the decimal point always comes after the ones place, even if it is not written there.

Metric Units

Preview Key Ideas

Briefly preview the key ideas of the lesson in the students' primary language so that students can better comprehend the English instruction.

Para convertir entre unidades métricas, multiplicamos o dividimos por una potencia de 10. Pensar acerca de cuántas unidades pequeñas hay en cada unidad grande puede ayudarnos a convertir entre las unidades.	To convert between metric units, we multiply or divide by a power of 10. Thinking about how many smaller units are in each larger unit can help us convert between units.

Access Vocabulary

Before or during the lesson, be sure to clarify the words below:

convert (*Student Edition* p. 404) to change one thing into another
unfolded (*Student Edition* p. 404) opened or spread out

Spanish Cognates

These words take advantage of what students and their families may know in their home language in order to accelerate the acquisition of math concepts in English.

decimeter decímetro
convert convertir
meter metro

Review Key Ideas

Have students complete the activity below to make sure that they understand the lesson concept. Have students work in pairs.

Haz una tabla de medidas de diferentes partes del cuerpo para compararlas. Incluye medidas de tu cuello, tu cintura, la extensión de tu brazo y el largo de tu brazo desde el hombro hasta los dedos de tu mano. Discute con tu compañero(a) si alguna de estas medidas son casi parecidas o son las mismas.	Make a chart to compare measurements of different body parts. Include measurements for your neck, your wrist, your arm span, and your arm length from shoulder to fingertips. Discuss whether any of these measurements are close or the same.

Metric Measurements of Length

Preview Key Ideas

Briefly preview the key ideas of the lesson in the students' primary language so that students can better comprehend the English instruction.

En esta lección mediremos longitudes entre el sistema métrico y expresaremos medidas métricas como los decimales de algunas unidades.	In this lesson we will measure lengths within the metric system and express metric measurements as decimals of common units.

Access Vocabulary

Before or during the lesson, be sure to clarify the words below:

prescription (*Teacher's Edition Vol 2* p. 409A) a rule or a direction
express (*Student Edition* p. 406) show, indicate, or represent
firehouse (*Student Edition* p. 406) sometimes called the *fire station,* a place where the fire trucks and fire fighters stay when they are not fighting a fire or attending to some other emergency

Spanish Cognates

These words take advantage of what students and their families may know in their home language in order to accelerate the acquisition of math concepts in English.

metric métrica
groups grupos
monitor monitor

Review Key Ideas

Have students complete the activity below to make sure that they understand the lesson concept. Have students work in small groups.

Con tu grupo, discute acerca de si eres más alto en pulgadas o en centímetros. Explica por qué piensas que tu respuesta es correcta.	Discuss whether you are taller in inches or in centimeters. Explain why you think your answer is correct.

Adding and Subtracting Decimals

Preview Key Ideas

Briefly preview the key ideas of the lesson in the students' primary language so that students can better comprehend the English instruction.

En esta lección practicaremos a sumar y a sustraer decimales. Sumar y sustraer decimales es similar a sumar y a sustraer cantidades de dinero.	In this lesson we will practice adding and subtracting decimals. Adding and subtracting decimals is similar to adding and subtracting amounts of money.

Access Vocabulary

Before or during the lesson, be sure to clarify the words below:

barefoot (*Student Edition* p. 413) without shoes on your feet
lap (*Student Edition* p. 413) one time around a race course
freestyle (*Student Edition* p. 413) a swim stroke sometimes called the crawl
marathon (*Student Edition* p. 413) a long-distance race of about 26 miles
aligning (*Teacher's Edition Vol 2* p. 410B) bringing into line; lining up two or more items
steeplechase (*Student Edition* p. 413) a race on a course that has barriers, ditches, and other obstacles over which contestants must jump

Spanish Cognates

These words take advantage of what students and their families may know in their home language in order to accelerate the acquisition of math concepts in English.

Olympics olímpicos
event evento
marathon maratón

Review Key Ideas

Have students complete the activity below to make sure that they understand the lesson concept.

Explica y enseña un ejemplo de por qué es importante alinear los puntos decimales cuando sumamos cantidades de dinero.	Explain and show an example of why it is important to line up the decimal points when adding money.

Using Decimals

Preview Key Ideas

Briefly preview the key ideas of the lesson in the students' primary language so that students can better comprehend the English instruction.

En esta lección vamos a sumar y a sustraer decimales para resolver problemas. Hay muchas situaciones que implican números decimales.	In this lesson we will add and subtract decimals to solve problems. Many different situations involve decimal numbers.

Access Vocabulary

Before or during the lesson, be sure to clarify the terms and phrases below:

alternates (*Teacher's Edition Vol 2* p. 418–419) switches between; takes turns
used car (*Student Edition* p. 418) a car that has been owned and used by someone else
award the difference (*Student Edition* p. 419) give the remainder to the winner
running a tab (*Teacher's Edition Vol 2* p. 418B) setting up a bill to be paid at the end of a period of time

Spanish Cognates

These words take advantage of what students and their families may know in their home language in order to accelerate the acquisition of math concepts in English.

miles millas
reasoning razonamiento
odometer odómetro
alternates alternar

Review Key Ideas

Have students complete the activity below to make sure that they understand the lesson concept. Have students work in pairs.

Escribe dos problemas narrativos usando decimales. Haz que tu compañero(a) los corrija y trate de solucionarlos. Comparte tus problemas narrativos con otro grupo de estudiantes. Selecciona el mejor e ilústralo.	Write two word problems using decimals. Have your partner check them and try to solve them. Share your word problems with other pairs of students. Select the best one and illustrate it.

Balancing a Checkbook

Preview Key Ideas

Briefly preview the key ideas of the lesson in the students' primary language so that students can better comprehend the English instruction.

En esta lección veremos como sumar y sustraer es muy útil en aplicaciones practicas como el balancear una chequera. Cuando balanceas una chequera, tú sabes cuánto dinero tienes en tu cuenta de cheques.	In this lesson we will see how adding and subtracting decimals is useful in practical applications such as balancing a checkbook. When we balance a checkbook, we learn how much money we have in our checking account.

Access Vocabulary

Before or during the lesson, be sure to clarify the terms below:

balancing (*Student Edition* p. 420) computing the difference between the debits and credits of an account
transactions (*Student Edition* p. 420) records of bank account withdrawals and deposits
checkbook register (*Student Edition* p. 420) a book for recording bank account transactions
statement (*Student Edition* p. 421) printed report of a bank account telling what has been deposited and withdrawn

Spanish Cognates

These words take advantage of what students and their families may know in their home language in order to accelerate the acquisition of math concepts in English.

transaction transacción
credit crédito
check register registro de cheques
deposit depósito

Review Key Ideas

Have students complete the activity below to make sure that they understand the lesson concept.

Entrevista a una persona adulta que tenga una cuenta de cheques. Pregúntale que método él o ella utiliza para corregir los errores cuando el balance de la chequera no coincide con el estado de cuentas del banco.	Interview an adult with a checking account. Ask what method he or she uses to correct checkbook errors when the checkbook balance does not match the bank statement.

Multiplying by a Whole Number

Preview Key Ideas

Briefly preview the key ideas of the lesson in the students' primary language so that students can better comprehend the English instruction.

En esta lección encontraremos el producto de un decimal y de un número entero. Podemos usar lo que sabemos acerca de la multiplicación de números enteros y acerca de la posición del valor para multiplicar decimales.	In this lesson we will find the product of a decimal and a whole number. We will use what we know about multiplying whole numbers and about place value to multiply decimals.

Access Vocabulary

Before or during the lesson, be sure to clarify the terms below:

color guard (*Student Edition* p. 424) an honor guard; flag or standard carriers
cloth (*Student Edition* p. 424) fabric; material that can be cut and sewn
unison (*Teacher's Edition Vol 2* p. 424B) voicing the same words at the same time

Spanish Cognates

These words take advantage of what students and their families may know in their home language in order to accelerate the acquisition of math concepts in English.

multiplications multiplicaciones
decimal factor factor decimal
electrical eléctrico
invitation invitación

Review Key Ideas

Have students complete the activity below to make sure that they understand the lesson concept. Have students work in pairs.

Escribe problemas de multiplicación con un decimal y un número entero. Intercambia tus problemas con tu compañero(a). Determina los límites de cada problema. Resuelve los problemas y revisa que tus respuestas estén entre los límites.	Write four multiplication problems each with a decimal and a whole number. Trade problems with your partner. Determine the boundaries for each problem. Solve the problems, and check that your answers fall between the boundaries.

Graphing and Applying Decimals

Preview Key Ideas

Briefly preview the key ideas of the lesson in the students' primary language so that students can better comprehend the English instruction.

En esta lección practicaremos a aplicar las reglas de funciones y a graficar decimales y fracciones. Los puntos con las coordenadas decimales pueden ser mostrados en una gráfica.	In this lesson we will practice applying function rules and graphing decimals and fractions. Points with decimal coordinates can be shown on a graph.

Access Vocabulary

Before or during the lesson, be sure to clarify the terms below:

x-value (*Teacher's Edition Vol 2* p. 428–429) the number, point, or value from the horizontal axis of a graph

y-value (*Teacher's Edition Vol 2* p. 428B) the number, point, or value from the vertical axis of a graph

look ahead (*Teacher's Edition Vol 2* p. 428B) preview the information that you will study in the next lesson

chart (*Student Edition* p. 428) a table, graph, or diagram

point (*Student Edition* p. 428) a precise position

Spanish Cognates

These words take advantage of what students and their families may know in their home language in order to accelerate the acquisition of math concepts in English.

graph gráfica
coordinates coordenadas
gallon galón

Review Key Ideas

Have students complete the activity below to make sure that they understand the lesson concept. Have students work in pairs.

Con tu compañero(a) crea una máquina de funciones con una regla que implique multiplicar un decimal. Túrnense para introducir números de entrada y calcular el número de salida. Hagan una gráfica de los números de salida.	Create a function machine with a rule that involves multiplying a decimal. Take turns inputting whole numbers and computing the output. Graph the outputs.

Metric Units of Weight and Volume

Preview Key Ideas

Briefly preview the key ideas of the lesson in the students' primary language so that students can better comprehend the English instruction.

Podemos medir objetos para hallar su peso y volumen. El peso describe cuán pesado es un objeto. El volumen mide el espacio adentro de un objeto. Practicaremos a convertir pesos y volúmenes del sistema métrico.	We can measure objects to find their weight and volume. Weight describes how heavy something is. Volume measures the space inside an object. We will practice converting weights and volumes within the metric system.

Access Vocabulary

Before or during the lesson, be sure to clarify the terms below:

graph (*Student Edition* p. 431) to plot on a graph
line graph (*Student Edition* p. 431) a graph of points connected by a broken line
graph paper (*Teacher's Edition Vol 2* p. 430B) paper ruled in small squares or other units on which graphs, charts, and diagrams can be drawn
plot (*English Learner Support Guide* p. 106) to make a diagram, chart, or graph and fill it with information

Spanish Cognates

These words take advantage of what students and their families may know in their home language in order to accelerate the acquisition of math concepts in English.

experiment experimento
result resultado

Review Key Ideas

Have students complete the activity below to make sure that they understand the lesson concept. Have students work in pairs.

Haz una lista de las abreviaciones de peso del sistema métrico. Recuerda que la unidad básica del peso es el gramo (g). Explica la diferencia entre peso y volumen y cuáles unidades se usan para cada uno.	Make a chart of the abbreviations for weights in the metric system. Remember that the basic unit of weight is the gram (g). Explain the difference between weight and volume and name the units used for each.

Cubic Centimeters

Preview Key Ideas

Briefly preview the key ideas of the lesson in the students' primary language so that students can better comprehend the English instruction.

En esta lección exploraremos el centímetro cúbico como una unidad de volumen del sistema métrico. El volumen mide el espacio adentro de un objeto.	In this lesson we will explore the cubic centimeter as a metric unit of volume. Volume measures the space inside an object.

Access Vocabulary

Before or during the lesson, be sure to clarify the words below:

cube (*Student Edition* p. 432) a regular solid with six square sides
drawer (*Student Edition* p. 433) a box with an open top that slides into a piece of furniture
garage (*Student Edition* p. 433) a shelter for cars

Spanish Cognates

These words take advantage of what students and their families may know in their home language in order to accelerate the acquisition of math concepts in English.

cubic cúbico
volume volumen
identical idéntico

Review Key Ideas

Have students complete the activity below to make sure that they understand the lesson concept.

Haz un resumen escrito de lo que has aprendido acerca del sistema métrico. Da ejemplos de unidades que se usan para medir longitud, peso y volumen.	Write a summary of what you have learned about the metric system. Give examples of units used for the measurement of length, weight, and volume.

Lines

Preview Key Ideas

Briefly preview the key ideas of the lesson in the students' primary language so that students can better comprehend the English instruction.

Esta lección nos presentará algunos nuevos términos como: **segmento de recta, semirrecta y vértice.** *En español, a straight line en las matemáticas se llama una* **recta.** *Vamos a ver las relaciones que existen entre una recta, los puntos y los ángulos. Por ejemplo, veremos que los ángulos están formados por segmentos de recta con un punto común que se llama* **vértice.**	This lesson will introduce some new terms: *line, segment, ray,* and *vertex.* In Spanish, a straight line is called a *recta* in mathematics. We will look at the relationships among lines, points, and angles. For example, we will see that angles are formed by line segments with a common endpoint called a *vertex.*

Access Vocabulary

Before or during the lesson, be sure to clarify the terms below:

forever (*Student Edition* p. 448) without finish, having no end
half line (*Student Edition* p. 448) a ray, a line segment that extends forever in the other direction from an endpoint
point (*Student Edition* p. 448) an exact location in space

Spanish Cognates

These words take advantage of what students and their families may know in their home language in order to accelerate the acquisition of math concepts in English.

segment segmento
points puntos
geometry geometría

Review Key Ideas

Have students complete the activity below to make sure that they understand the lesson concept.

Dibuja en una hoja tres secciones para mostrar y explicar la diferencia que existe entre una recta, un segmento de recta y una semirrecta. Busca el significado de estos términos en un diccionario bilingüe de inglés y de tu idioma nativo.	Draw a three-panel drawing to show and explain the difference between a line, a line segment, and a ray. Look up these terms in a bilingual dictionary of English and your home language.

Angles

Preview Key Ideas

Briefly preview the key ideas in the lesson in the students' primary language so that students can better comprehend the English instruction.

Hoy vamos a aprender acerca de los ángulos rectos, obtusos y agudos. Aprenderemos a pensar en los ángulos como parte de una rotación. También aprenderemos cómo usar un transportador para medir el tamaño de un ángulo. Es muy importante saber cómo usar el transportador para cuando quieras replicar un ángulo exactamente.	Today we will learn about angles—*right angles, obtuse,* and *acute angles.* We will learn to think about angles as a part of a rotation. We will also learn how to use a protractor to measure the size of an angle. This will be important to learn in order to replicate an angle exactly.

Access Vocabulary

Before or during the lesson, be sure to clarify the words and phrases below:

degree (*Teacher's Edition Vol 2* p. 450B) unit of measurement used for temperature and for size of angles

straightedge (*Teacher's Edition Vol 2* p. 450B) rectangular bar with a straight edge used for drawing straight lines

treasure hunt (*Student Edition* p. 450) a game where the point is to find hidden items

right angle (*Student Edition* p. 452) an angle that is 90°; Many EL students know the word *right* to mean "the opposite of wrong."

acute angle (*Student Edition* p. 452) an angle which measures between 0° and 90°

obtuse angle (*Student Edition* p. 452) an angle that is greater than 90°

patted down (*Student Edition* p. 450) tapped gently to make smooth or flat

Spanish Cognates

These words take advantage of what students and their families may know in their home language in order to accelerate the acquisition of math concepts in English.

angle ángulo
vertex vértice
complete completo

Review Key Ideas

Have students complete the activity below to make sure that they understand the lesson concept.

Explica por qué crees que solo medimos los ángulos hasta 180 grados.	Explain why angles are usually only measured up to 180 degrees.

Parallel, Perpendicular, and Intersecting Lines

Preview Key Ideas

Briefly preview the key ideas in the lesson in the students' primary language so that students can better comprehend the English instruction.

En esta lección aprenderemos acerca de tres diferentes tipos de rectas. Dos rectas son perpendiculares cuando se intersectan entre sí para formar ángulos rectos. Las rectas paralelas son rectas que van en la misma dirección y permanecen equidistantes en todos los puntos. Las rectas paralelas, también se mantienen en la misma distancia entre sí no importa que tan largas sean. Las rectas secantes son rectas que intersectan entre sí, como las calles que se juntan en una intersección.	In this lesson we will learn about three different types of lines. *Perpendicular lines* are intersecting lines that meet to form right angles. *Parallel lines* are lines that go in the same direction and never meet. They remain the same distance apart no matter how far they are extended. *Intersecting lines* are lines that meet, like streets that cross at an intersection.

Access Vocabulary

Before or during the lesson, be sure to clarify the words and phrase below:

plane (*Student Edition* p. 454) a flat surface; EL students may know the word *plane* as another word for "airplane."
in each case (*Student Edition* p. 454) in every example
intersecting (*Teacher's Edition Vol 2* p. 454B) going or cutting across; crossing paths

Spanish Cognates

These words take advantage of what students and their families may know in their home language in order to accelerate the acquisition of math concepts in English.

parallel paralelo
perpendicular perpendicular
pair par

Review Key Ideas

Have students complete the activity below to make sure that they understand the lesson concept.

Con tu compañero(a), haz una lista ilustrada con tres ejemplos de rectas perpendiculares que se encuentra en la vida cotidiana. Haz una lista e ilustra los ejemplos.	Work with a partner to come up with at least three examples of perpendicular lines you encounter in daily life. Make a list and illustrate the examples.

Quadrilaterals and Other Polygons

Preview Key Ideas

Briefly preview the key ideas in lesson in the students' primary language so that students can better comprehend the English instruction.

En esta lección vamos a aprender acerca de unos polígonos o formas cuyos nombres nos dicen cuántos lados tiene la figura. También aprendemos sobre algunos cuadriláteros, cuyo nombre viene de una raíz latina y significa con cuatro lados.	In this lesson we are going to learn about several polygons, or shapes whose names tell how many sides the figure has. We will also learn about *quadrilaterals*, a word which comes from a Latin root that means "four sides."

Access Vocabulary

Before or during the lesson, be sure to clarify the term below:

plane figure (*Teacher's Edition Vol 2* p. 456B) two-dimensional figure, a shape that can only be measured by height and width.

Spanish Cognates

These words take advantage of what students and their families may know in their home language in order to accelerate the acquisition of math concepts in English.

polygon polígono
characteristics características

Review Key Ideas

Have students complete the activity below to make sure that they understand the lesson concept.

Dibuja cada figura que estudiamos en esta lección. Al lado de cada uno dibuja un objeto que sabes que tenga esa forma. [Respuesta posible: La señal de tráfico Stop tiene la figura de octágono.]	Draw each of the shapes that are introduced in this lesson. Next to each shape draw a picture of some object that you know that has that shape. [Possible answer: A stop sign is in the shape of an octagon.]

Triangles

Preview Key Ideas

Briefly preview the key ideas of the lesson in the students' primary language so that students can better comprehend the English instruction.

La lección de hoy trata de los triángulos. Un polígono de tres lados es un triángulo. Hay diferentes tipos de triángulos. Hay un triángulo equilátero *que tiene tres lados de la misma medida. Un* triángulo isósceles *tiene dos lados iguales. El* triángulo escaleno *tiene los tres lados de diferentes longitudes. Un* triángulo recto *tiene un ángulo recto. El* triángulo agudo *tiene tres ángulos agudos y un* triángulo obtuso *tiene un ángulo obtuso. Veamos las figuras que están en sus libros.*	In today's lesson we are going to learn about triangles. A polygon that has three sides is a triangle. There are different types of triangles. An *equilateral triangle* has three sides which are all the same length. An *isosceles triangle* has two sides which are the same length. The sides of a *scalene triangle* are different lengths. A *right triangle* is a triangle that has a right angle. An *acute triangle* has three acute angles, and an *obtuse triangle* has one obtuse angle. See the pictures in the **Student Edition.**

Access Vocabulary

Before or during the lesson, be sure to clarify the terms below:

rubber bands (*Teacher's Edition Vol 2* p. 458B) stretchy loops of rubber or elastic used to hold objects together

geoboard (*Teacher's Edition Vol 2* p. 458A) plastic square board with equally spaced prongs, used to form geometric shapes with rubber bands that are stretched and wrapped around the prongs

real-life (*English Learner Support Guide* p. 112) happening or appearing in everyday life

Spanish Cognates

These words take advantage of what students and their families may know in their home language in order to accelerate the acquisition of math concepts in English.

angles ángulos
triangles triángulos

Review Key Ideas

Have students complete the activity below to make sure that they understand the lesson concept.

Dibuja y etiqueta unos ejemplos de las seis clases de triángulos. Dibuja dos ejemplos de algo que se encuentra en la vida cotidiana que tengan estas formas. [Respuesta posible: un banderín, una señal para los peatones escolares o un azulejo.]	Draw and label six types of triangles. Draw a real-life example of two of these shapes. [Possible answers: a pennant, a school crossing sign, or a floor tile.]

Circles

Preview Key Ideas

Briefly preview the key ideas in the lesson in the students' primary language so that students can better comprehend the English instruction.

En esta lección vamos a aprender más acerca de los círculos y las partes de los círculos. Es importante saber los nombres de las partes de los círculos, así como: **radio, diámetro, cuerda y circunferencia.**	In this lesson we will learn more about circles and the parts of circles. It is important to know the parts of circles such as *radius, diameter, chord,* and *circumference.*

Access Vocabulary

Before or during the lesson, be sure to clarify the phrase below:

path around the circle (*Teacher's Edition Vol 2* p. 460B) measured route all the way around the circle

Spanish Cognates

These words take advantage of what students and their families may know in their home language in order to accelerate the acquisition of math concepts in English.

segment segmento
center centro

Review Key Ideas

Have students complete the activity below to make sure that they understand the lesson concept.

Con tu grupo, explica cómo son similares las palabras **círculo y circunferencia.**	Work together to explain how the words *circle* and *circumference* are similar.

Congruence and Similarity

Preview Key Ideas

Briefly preview the key ideas of the lesson in the students' primary language so that students can better comprehend the English instruction.

Hoy vamos a aprender sobre la congruencia. Dos figuras son congruentes si son iguales de forma y tamaño. Si una cabe exactamente encima de la otra, son congruentes. Si dos figuras tienen la misma forma pero no necesariamente el mismo tamaño, se dice que son similares.	Today we are going to learn about congruence. Two figures are congruent if they are the same size and same shape. If one fits exactly on top of another, they are congruent. If two figures are the same shape but not the same size, they are similar.

Access Vocabulary

Before or during the lesson, be sure to clarify the terms and phrase below:

map was blown up (*Teacher's Edition Vol 2* p. 466–467) map has been enlarged
picture frames (*Student Edition* p. 466) containers or structures that are used to display photographs or other images
factories (*Student Edition* p. 466) buildings or groups of buildings where goods are made
similar (*Student Edition* p. 466) alike; sharing some of the same characteristics

Spanish Cognates

These words take advantage of what students and their families may know in their home language in order to accelerate the acquisition of math concepts in English.

geometric geométrico
figures figuras
similar similar

Review Key Ideas

Have students complete the activity below to make sure that they understand the lesson concept.

Dobla una hoja de papel por la mitad. En un lado dibuja, etiqueta e ilustra tres objetos congruentes y en la otra mitad tres objetos similares.	Fold a sheet of paper in half. List, label, and illustrate three congruent objects on one half. On the other half of the sheet, illustrate three objects that are similar.

Rotation, Translation, and Reflection

Preview Key Ideas

Briefly preview the key ideas of the lesson in the students' primary language so that students can better comprehend the English instruction.

En esta lección vamos a ver cómo se ve una figura cuando la cambiamos de posiciones. Vamos a aprender cómo se llaman estos cambios de posición y vemos cómo en realidad las figuras no cambian.	In this lesson we are going to see how a figure appears to change and look different when we move it around in different ways. We will learn the names for these moves and will see how the shape really does not change.

Access Vocabulary

Before or during the lesson, be sure to clarify the terms below:

mirror image (*Student Edition* p. 468) image that is exactly the same only reversed like we would see if we looked at it in a mirror
flipping (*Student Edition* p. 468) turning over an object; moving a shape to an opposite position
reflection (*Teacher's Edition Vol 2* p. 468B) an image given back by a mirror or other surface
rotation (*Student Edition* p. 468) a complete turn

Spanish Cognates

These words take advantage of what students and their families may know in their home language in order to accelerate the acquisition of math concepts in English.

congruent congruente
translation traslación
reflection reflejo

NOTE: Although in English the math term for translation is the same as the word used to describe foreign language translation, in Spanish these are two different terms. In math it is *traslación;* for languages it is *traducción*.

Review Key Ideas

Have students complete the activity below to make sure that they understand the lesson concept.

Trabaja con tu compañero(a) para explicar cómo las rotaciones, traslaciones y reflexiones pueden usarse como métodos para determinar congruencia. Hay ejemplos en el libro que te pueden ayudar. En un papel, dibuja tres formas de modo que para cada forma haya un par de ejemplos congruentes y otro par que sean similares.	Work with a partner to explain how rotations, translations, and reflections can be used as methods to help determine congruence. There are examples in the book that can help you. Draw three shapes so that for each shape there is one pair of congruent shapes and one pair of similar shapes.

Lines of Symmetry

Preview Key Ideas

Briefly preview the key ideas of the lesson in the students' primary language so that students can better comprehend the English instruction.

En esta lección vamos a aprender que el eje de simetría de una figura corta la figura en dos partes que son el reflejo exacto entre sí. Es decir, el eje de simetría formará dos partes congruentes.	In this lesson we will learn that a line of symmetry in a figure cuts the figure into two parts that are mirror images of each other. That is, the line of symmetry will form two congruent parts.

Access Vocabulary

Before or during the lesson, be sure to clarify the words below:

unfold (*Student Edition* p. 470) open something that has been folded
infinite (*Student Edition* p. 471) without any end
equidistant (*Student Edition* p. 473) equal distance, two points that measure the same distance

Spanish Cognates

These words take advantage of what students and their families may know in their home language in order to accelerate the acquisition of math concepts in English.

vertical vertical
horizontal horizontal

Review Key Ideas

Have students complete the activity below to make sure that they understand the lesson concept.

Define el eje de simetría. Dibuja unas figuras, recórtalas y enseña el eje de simetría en cada figura.	Define *line of symmetry*. Draw shapes, cut them out, and show the line of symmetry in each shape.

Space Figures

Preview Key Ideas

Briefly preview the key ideas of the lesson in the students' primary language so that students can better comprehend the English instruction.

En esta lección aprendemos las propiedades de figuras geométricas y creamos e identificamos redes que se doblen para formar figuras geométricas.	In this lesson we will learn the names and properties of space figures and learn to create and identify nets that fold to become space figures.

Access Vocabulary

Before or during the lesson, be sure to clarify the words and phrases below:

faces (*Student Edition* p. 474) flat surfaces of space figures; Cubes have six congruent square faces. EL students may know *face* to mean "the human face."
base of a cylinder (*Student Edition* p. 474) The top and bottom of a cylinder are called *bases*.
everyday lives (*Student Edition* p. 474) a common or regular day

Spanish Cognates

These words take advantage of what students and their families may know in their home language in order to accelerate the acquisition of math concepts in English.

cylinder cilindro
cone cono

Review Key Ideas

Have students complete the activity below to make sure that they understand the lesson concept.

Usa una red para un cubo y explica o etiqueta cómo pudiste hacer una figura geométrica con ese material plano.	Use a net for a cube and explain or show how you were able to make a space figure out of flat material.

The Five Regular Polyhedra (Platonic Solids)

Preview Key Ideas

Briefly preview the key ideas of the lesson in the students' primary language so that students can better comprehend the English instruction.

En esta lección, vamos a aprender acerca de los poliedros, tales como los cubos, y vamos a aprender a identificarlos. Vamos a ver que son figuras geométricas con superficies planas. No son curvos como los conos, cilindros y esferas, que no son poliedros. Vamos a aprender a contar sus caras, vértices y aristas.	In this lesson we will learn about regular polyhedra, such as *cubes,* and learn to identify them. We will see that they are space figures with flat surfaces. They are not curved like *cones, cylinders,* and *spheres,* which are not polyhedra. We will learn to count their faces, vertices, and edges.

Access Vocabulary

Before or during the lesson, be sure to clarify the words and phrases below:

looks "funny" (*Teacher's Edition Vol 2* p. 478B) looks odd, unusual, unexpected
viewpoint (*Teacher's Edition Vol 2* p. 480–481) way to look at or consider an object or issue
hollow (*Student Edition* p. 479) having a hole or a space inside
how many . . . does it take (*Student Edition* p. 479) what number is required or necessary
patterns (*Student Edition* p. 480) designs that are repeated in some recognizable fashion

Spanish Cognates

These words take advantage of what students and their families may know in their home language in order to accelerate the acquisition of math concepts in English.

polyhedron poliedro
list lista
cylinder cilindro
cube cubo

Review Key Ideas

Have students complete the activity below to make sure that they understand the lesson concept.

Haz una lista de objetos sólidos que tengas en tu casa que sean como los que estudiaste en esta lección. Dibuja unos objetos y tráelos a la clase para compartirlos.	Make a list of things in your home that are examples of the solid objects you explored in this lesson. Draw pictures or bring to class some of these objects to share.

Pyramids and Prisms

Preview Key Ideas

Briefly preview the key ideas of the lesson in the students' primary language so that students can better comprehend the English instruction.

En esta lección vemos que hay varios tipos de pirámides. Aprenderemos que la pirámide es otro tipo de poliedro y que algunas pirámides tienen bases de diferentes formas que causan que la pirámide tenga diferentes números de caras, aristas y vértices.	In this lesson we see that there are several types of pyramids. We learn that a pyramid is another type of polyhedron, and that different pyramids have different shaped bases which cause the pyramid to have different numbers of faces, edges, and vertices.

Access Vocabulary

Before or during the lesson, be sure to clarify the words below:

models (*Teacher's Edition Vol 2* p. 482B) examples, usually built to look like the actual object in three dimensions, not flat like a drawing
net (*Student Edition* p. 483) a flat pattern that forms a geometric shape when it is folded

Spanish Cognates

These words take advantage of what students and their families may know in their home language in order to accelerate the acquisition of math concepts in English.

prism prisma
pyramid pirámide
model modelo

Review Key Ideas

Have students complete the activity below to make sure that they understand the lesson concept.

Trabaja con tu grupo para hacer una gráfica con el número de caras, aristas y vértices que tenga cada figura geométrica. Empieza con la figura geométrica que tenga sólo un vértice y ni una arista.	Work in small groups to create a chart that shows the number of faces, edges, and vertices each space figure has. Start with the space figure that has one vertex and no edges.

Calculating Area

Preview Key Ideas

Briefly preview the key ideas of the lesson in the students' primary language so that students can better comprehend the English instruction.

En esta lección estimamos el área de una figura empleando una cuadrícula. También repasamos cómo encontrar el área de un cuadrado y un rectángulo. Determinamos el área de una figura compuesta. Una figura compuesta está hecha de dos o más formas.	In this lesson we will estimate the area of a figure using a grid. We will also review how to find the area of a square and a rectangle. We will find the area of a compound figure. A compound figure is a figure made up of more than one shape.

Access Vocabulary

Before or during the lesson, be sure to clarify the terms below:

compound figure (*Teacher's Edition Vol 2* p. 486B) a figure made up of two or more other figures—such as a big rectangle with a small rectangle joined to one side
grid (*Teacher's Edition Vol 2* p. 486B) a pattern of intersecting, or crossing, lines that divides a chart into small squares
trade papers (*Teacher's Edition Vol 2* p. 486B) exchange worksheets with another student
shaded figure (*Student Edition* p. 486) shape that is darkened to show a contrast

Spanish Cognates

These words take advantage of what students and their families may know in their home language in order to accelerate the acquisition of math concepts in English.

perimeter perímetro
area área
strategy estrategia

Review Key Ideas

Have students complete the activity below to make sure that they understand the lesson concept.

Trabaja con tu compañero(a) para describir dos maneras diferentes de calcular el área de una figura. Dibuja un ejemplo y haz una lista de direcciones paso a paso.	Work with a partner to describe two different ways to calculate the area of a figure. Draw an example and list step-by-step directions.

Measuring and Calculating Perimeter

Preview Key Ideas

Briefly preview key ideas of the lesson in the students' primary language so that students can better comprehend the English instruction.

Esta lección nos enseña que se puede encontrar el perímetro de una figura aún cuando no tenemos las medidas de longitudes de los lados. Recuerda que el perímetro es la distancia alrededor de la figura. También vemos que se puede determinar el perímetro si sabemos el área de la figura y la medida de longitud de uno de sus lados. Recuerden que el área es el número de unidades cuadradas encerradas por una figura.	This lesson shows us that we can still find the perimeter of a figure when we don't have the measurements of the lengths of the sides. Remember that perimeter is the distance around a figure. We will also see that we can determine the perimeter if we know the area of a figure and length of one of its sides. Remember that the area is the number of square units inside a figure.

Access Vocabulary

Before or during the lesson, be sure to clarify the terms below:

graph paper (*Student Edition* p. 489) paper with equal squares marked on it to make it easier to draw shapes, graphs, and straight lines
tool (*Teacher's Edition Vol 2* p. 488B) anything that is used to complete a problem or task
explore (*Teacher's Edition Vol 2* p. 488B) investigate or try to discover through careful study

Spanish Cognates

These words take advantage of what students and their families may know in their home language in order to accelerate the acquisition of math concepts in English.

to calculate calcular
perimeter perímetro
equivalent equivalente

Review Key Ideas

Have students complete the activity below to make sure that they understand the lesson concept.

Con tu compañero(a) completa una gráfica de dos columnas para demostrar cómo están relacionados el perímetro y área y cómo son diferentes.	Work with a partner to complete a two-column chart that describes how perimeter and area are related and how they are different.

Dividing by a One-Digit Divisor

Preview Key Ideas

Briefly preview the key ideas of the lesson in the students' primary language so that students can better comprehend the English instruction.

En esta lección vamos a aprender a dividir un número por un divisor de un dígito. Recuerda que la división es el inverso de la multiplicación.	In this lesson we will learn how to divide a number by a one-digit divisor. Don't forget that division is the inverse of multiplication.

Access Vocabulary

Before or during the lesson, be sure to clarify the terms and phrases below:

seven-way split (*Student Edition* p. 504) to divide something among seven people
keep a record (*Student Edition* p. 504) write down the way they divided the money so that they can remember
person in charge (*Student Edition* p. 504) a person in a position of authority or responsibility; a person in command
lost-and-found (*Student Edition* p. 504) a place to hold items that have been recovered to be claimed by the people who originally misplaced them

Spanish Cognates

These words take advantage of what students and their families may know in their home language in order to accelerate the acquisition of math concepts in English.

divisor divisor
division división
department departamento

Review Key Ideas

Have students complete the activity below to make sure that they understand the lesson concept.

Con tu compañero(a) haz una muestra de una división con una descripción de cómo se divide. En el cartel explica todos los pasos y procedimientos de cómo poner el cociente en la línea del cociente, una explicación de cómo el divisor divide el dividendo en partes iguales y cómo se usa la sustracción.	Work with a partner to make a poster describing how to divide. On your poster, label all the important steps and procedures. Include placing quotients on the quotient line, explaining how the divisor splits the dividend into equal parts, and how subtraction is used.

Division: Written Form

Preview Key Ideas

Briefly preview the key ideas of the lesson in the students' primary language so that students can better comprehend the English instruction.

En esta lección entenderemos más el algoritmo de división. También, desarrollamos un procedimiento más corto para la división.	In this lesson we will begin to understand more of the division algorithm. We will also develop a shorter procedure for dividing.

Access Vocabulary

Before or during the lesson, be sure to clarify the terms below:

key (*Teacher's Edition Vol 2* p. 508–509) button on a calculator
vacation spot (*Teacher's Edition Vol 2* p. 508–509) vacation destination, place
inverse relationship (*Teacher's Edition Vol 2* p. 508B) one operation undoes the other
rather than (*Teacher's Edition Vol 2* p. 508B) instead of

Spanish Cognates

These words take advantage of what students and their families may know in their home language in order to accelerate the acquisition of math concepts in English.

dividend dividendo
quotient cociente
to distribute distribuir

Review Key Ideas

Have students complete the activity below to make sure that they understand the lesson concept.

Escribe un ejemplo de una división corta y etiqueta el dividendo, divisor, cociente y el resto. Piensa en tres cosas en la vida cotidiana que tengamos que dividir.	Write down a short form division example and label the dividend, divisor, quotient, and remainder. Think of three things that we have to divide in our daily lives.

Checking Division

Preview Key Ideas

Briefly preview the key ideas of the lesson in the students' primary language so that students can better comprehend the English instruction.

En esta lección tendremos más práctica dividiendo por divisores de un dígito, repasaremos la relación inversa entre la multiplicación y la división. Recuerda que la multiplicación deshace la división. También practicaremos el algoritmo de división encontrando dígitos que faltan en ejercicios ya hechos.	In this lesson we will get more practice dividing by one-digit divisors. We will review the inverse relationship between multiplication and division. Remember that multiplication undoes division. We will also practice the division algorithm by finding missing digits in already worked exercises.

Access Vocabulary

Before or during the lesson, be sure to clarify the term and phrase below:

flash cards (*Teacher's Edition Vol 2* p. 510–511) cards with math facts on them used to increase fast response in a flash or quick look at the fact
What's left? (*Teacher's Edition Vol 2* p. 510–511) amount that remains

Spanish Cognates

These words take advantage of what students and their families may know in their home language in order to accelerate the acquisition of math concepts in English.

divisor divisor
quotient cociente

Review Key Ideas

Have students complete the activity below to make sure that they understand the lesson concept.

Trabaja con tu compañero(a) para hacer un ejemplo de la estrategia que puede ser usada para revisar las respuestas en exámenes de selección múltiple. No te olvides multiplicar el divisor por el cociente y sumar cualquier resto. Luego, selecciona la respuesta que iguala el producto o suma.	Work with a partner. Use the checking-answer strategy to make an example that can be used on a multiple choice test. Remember to multiply the divisor by the quotient and add any remainder. Then select the multiple choice item that equals the product.

Division: Short Form

Preview Key Ideas

Briefly preview the key ideas of the lesson in the students' primary language so that students can better comprehend the English instruction.

En esta lección vamos a aprender un método más corto de apuntar las divisiones y practicamos a comprobar la división por la multiplicación.	In this lesson we will learn a shorter method of keeping division records and we will practice checking division by multiplying.

Access Vocabulary

Before or during the lesson, be sure to clarify the terms below:

short form (*Student Edition* p. 514) a way to divide with fewer steps
standard form (*Teacher's Edition Vol 2* p. 514B) common, step-by-step way to divide
jumping jacks (*Student Edition* p. 515) an exercise that involves hopping from a standing position, spreading the legs and placing the hands together over the head, then hopping again and returning to the first position
circulation (*Teacher's Edition Vol 2* p. 514–515) In this lesson, *circulation* refers to the movement of paper and coin money from one person to another.

Spanish Cognates

These words take advantage of what students and their families may know in their home language in order to accelerate the acquisition of math concepts in English.

division división
algorithm algoritmo
method método
to prefer preferir

Review Key Ideas

Have students complete the activity below to make sure that they understand the lesson concept.

Haz una tabla de dos columnas y escribe las diferencias y similitudes entre la forma estándar y la forma corta de la división.	Make a two-column chart, and list the differences and similarities between the standard form and the short form of division.

Division Patterns

Preview Key Ideas

Briefly preview the key of the lesson ideas in the students' primary language so that students can better comprehend the English instruction.

En esta lección practicaremos a dividir con divisores de un dígito y vamos a ver cómo los patrones nos ayudan a encontrar las respuestas.	In this lesson we will practice dividing with one-digit divisors and see how patterns can help us find answers.

Access Vocabulary

Before or during the lesson, be sure to clarify the terms and phrase below:

darts (*Teacher's Edition Vol 2* p. 516–517) sharp, pointed metal you throw at a target
target (*Teacher's Edition Vol 2* p. 516–517) circle shaped goal to aim at in a dart game
Where did the darts land? (*Teacher's Edition Vol 2* p. 516–517) where the darts hit the target
fairly sure (*Teacher's Edition Vol 2* p. 516–517) somewhat or moderately believing in something; having some confidence

Spanish Cognates

These words take advantage of what students and their families may know in their home language in order to accelerate the acquisition of math concepts in English.

pattern patrón
concept concepto
dinosaur dinosaurio

Review Key Ideas

Have students complete the activity below to make sure that they understand the lesson concept. Have students work in groups of three.

En el juego de los dardos, el jugador tiene que apuntar a un punto medio. Piensa en otros juegos, equipos deportivos o competencias individuales y trabaja con tu grupo para hacer una lista de lo que llamamos punto medio u objetivo en cada juego. [Respuestas posibles: gol, línea de meta, base de juego, canastas, línea de gol o bingo]	In the game of darts, the player has to aim at a target. Think of other games, team sports, and individual contests. In your groups, make a list of terms which refer to the target, objective, or purpose in each game. [Possible answers: goal, finish line, run or homerun, basket, checkmate, bingo]

Prime and Composite Numbers

Preview Key Ideas

Briefly preview the key of the lesson ideas in the students' primary language so that students can better comprehend the English instruction.

En esta lección aprenderemos que un número primo tiene solo dos factores y que los números compuestos tienen más de dos factores. También repasaremos cómo factorizar números.	In this lesson we will learn that a prime number has only two factors and composite numbers have more than two factors. We will also review factoring.

Access Vocabulary

Before or during the lesson, be sure to clarify the words below:

arrays (*Teacher's Edition Vol 2* p. 518–519) rectangular arrangement of quantities in rows and columns
orientation (*Student Edition* p. 518) the process of positioning or determining the position for something or someone

Spanish Cognates

These words take advantage of what students and their families may know in their home language in order to accelerate the acquisition of math concepts in English.

prime numbers números primos
illustration ilustración
orientation orientación

Review Key Ideas

Have students complete the activity below to make sure that they understand the lesson concept.

Da la definición de números primos y números compuestos. Explica si el número 1 es un número primo o un número compuesto y por qué.	Give the definitions of a prime number and a composite number. Tell whether *1* is a prime or composite number. Explain your answer.

Finding Factors

Preview Key Ideas

Briefly preview the key ideas of the lesson in the students' primary language so that students can better comprehend the English instruction.

En esta lección vamos a repasar y reconocer varios métodos de decidir si un número tiene factores de 2, 5, 10, 3, 9 u 11. Descubrimos que si sabemos las reglas de divisibilidad y los cuadrados, que hay solo un número compuesto menos que 100 que obviamente no es compuesto.	In this lesson we will recall and recognize various ways to decide whether a number has factors of 2, 5, 10, 3, 9, or 11. We will also discover that if we know the rules of divisibility and the square facts, there is only one composite number less than 100 that is not obviously composite.

Access Vocabulary

Before or during the lesson, be sure to clarify the terms below:

sense of numbers (*Teacher's Edition Vol 2* p. 520A) a feel for how numbers work, including an understanding of the connections between numbers, operations, and patterns
mathematicians (*Student Edition* p. 521) an expert in mathematics
quilt (*Student Edition* p. 521) a bed covering consisting of two pieces of cloth filled with soft stuffing material
arrange (*Student Edition* p. 521) put in proper order

Spanish Cognates

These words take advantage of what students and their families may know in their home language in order to accelerate the acquisition of math concepts in English.

factor factor
divisible divisible
mathematician matemático
direction dirección
situation situación

Review Key Ideas

Have students complete the activity below to make sure that they understand the lesson concept.

Trabaja con tu compañero(a) para crear un modelo de la regla que dice que todos los números pares son divisibles por 2. La palabra divisible se escribe y significa lo mismo en inglés y en español. ¿Puedes encontrar otras palabras que terminen en -ible que se escriban y signifiquen lo mismo en inglés y en español?	Work with a partner to create a model of the rule that all even numbers are divisible by 2. The word divisible is the same in English and in Spanish. Can you find any other words that end with *-ible* that are the same in English and Spanish?

Unit Cost

Preview Key Ideas

Briefly preview the key of the lesson ideas in the students' primary language so that students can better comprehend the English instruction.

En esta lección practicaremos a usar la división para encontrar el costo por unidad de algunos objetos y decidiremos cuál compra nos ahorrará dinero. También trabajaremos para desarrollar un sentido numérico en respuesta a cuánto dinero se gastó.	In this lesson we will practice using division to find unit costs of items and decide which purchases will save money. We will also work to develop our sense of numbers in response to how money is spent.

Access Vocabulary

Before or during the lesson, be sure to clarify the terms below:

better buy (*Student Edition* p. 526) the item that is the best value, good quality at the lowest price

cost effective (*Teacher's Edition Vol 2* p. 526A) not spending too much for an item, getting good value for the money

purchases (*Teacher's Edition Vol 2* p. 526A) items received by paying money for them

food pyramid (*Teacher's Edition Vol 2* p. 526–527) a diagram showing human nutritional needs

pertinent (*Teacher's Edition Vol 2* p. 526–527) connected to or having to do with the matter at hand

Spanish Cognates

These words take advantage of what students and their families may know in their home language in order to accelerate the acquisition of math concepts in English.

unit cost costo por unidad
calcium calcio
carton cartón
yogurt yogur

Review Key Ideas

Have students complete the activity below to make sure that they understand the lesson concept.

Explica el significado de los términos de costo por unidad y mejor compra y explica cómo se determina el costo por unidad. Usa el periódico para buscar anuncios o propagandas de supermercados que describan algunos productos, los cuáles puedas usar para encontrar el costo por unidad de cada uno de ellos y para determinar cuál sería la mejor compra.	Explain the meaning of the terms *unit cost* and *best buy*. Explain how to determine the unit cost. Use newspaper ads or store advertisements that show prices for groups of items. Find the unit cost and determine the better buy.

Using Inverses

Preview Key Ideas

Briefly preview the key ideas of the lesson in the students' primary language so that students can better comprehend the English instruction.

Hoy vamos a repasar la relación entre la multiplicación y la división. También, revisamos las funciones y el diagramar para ver cómo se usa una gráfica para solucionar problemas relacionados con la división.	Today we will review how multiplication and division are related. We will also review functions and graphing and see how to use a graph to solve related division problems.

Access Vocabulary

Before or during the lesson, be sure to clarify the terms and phrase below:

smoothie shop (*Student Edition* p. 528) restaurant that serves frozen fruit and yogurt drinks
undo (*Student Edition* p. 528) to reverse what has been done
it was off to the store (*Student Edition* p. 529) the plan or next step was to leave and go to the store
rework (*Teacher's Edition Vol 2* p. 531A) to work again; to do over again

Spanish Cognates
These words take advantage of what students and their families may know in their home language in order to accelerate the acquisition of math concepts in English.

inverse inverso
opposite opuesto
approximate aproximado

Review Key Ideas

Have students complete the activity below to make sure that they understand the lesson concept.

Diseña una divertida máquina de funciones y compártela con tu clase. Asegúrate que la máquina de funciones pueda hacer funciones inversas como una de sus propiedades.	Design a funny function machine and share it with the class. Make sure the machine can perform inverse functions as one of its settings.

Estimating Quotients

Preview Key Ideas

Briefly preview the key ideas of the lesson in the students' primary language so that students can better comprehend the English instruction.

En esta lección vamos a ver cómo usar estrategias de multiplicación para estimar cocientes en la división. Esto te ayudará a repasar tus divisiones y a ver si están correctas. Se puede estimar la respuesta a una división pensando en cuántas veces el divisor igualará el dividendo.	In this lesson we will see how to use multiplication strategies to estimate quotients. This will help us check our division to see if we are correct. We can estimate the answer to a division problem by thinking what number times the divisor will equal the dividend.

Access Vocabulary

Before or during the lesson, be sure to clarify the terms and phrase below:

pros and cons (*Teacher's Edition Vol 2* p. 532–533) positive and negative attributes
fertilizer (*Student Edition* p. 533) chemical or natural substance added to soil to make plants grow larger
new releases (*Student Edition* p. 533) items that have only been available for a short time in stores

Spanish Cognates

These words take advantage of what students and their families may know in their home language in order to accelerate the acquisition of math concepts in English.

estimation estimación
fertilizer fertilizante
opinion opinión

Review Key Ideas

Have students complete the activity below to make sure that they understand the lesson concept.

En la discusión guiada, nosotros hablamos acerca de cómo las respuestas matemáticas tienen que tener sentido. Vimos cómo la adición y la multiplicación son siempre posibles pero que la división y la sustracción no. Crea un ejemplo de un problema imposible y dibuja una ilustración para mostrar lo que piensas. Comparte tu ejemplo con tu clase.	In the Guided Discussion, we talked about how math answers need to make sense. We learned how addition and multiplication are always possible, but that division and subtraction are not. Create one example of an impossible problem and draw an illustration to show your thinking. Share your example with the class.

Dividing by a Two-Digit Divisor

Preview Key Ideas

Briefly preview the key ideas of the lesson in the students' primary language so that students can better comprehend the English instruction.

En esta lección aprendemos cómo dividir usando divisores de dos dígitos. Esto te ayudará a dividir números mayores.	In this lesson we will learn how to divide using a two-digit divisor. This will help us in dividing greater numbers.

Access Vocabulary

Before or during the lesson, be sure to clarify the phrases below:

jumping to a conclusion (*Teacher's Edition Vol 2* p. 534–535) to decide on an answer without considering all the facts or following the proper process
pass out (*Teacher's Edition Vol 2* p. 534B) to give away; distribute

Spanish Cognates

These words take advantage of what students and their families may know in their home language in order to accelerate the acquisition of math concepts in English.

divisor divisor
tangible tangible
different diferente
to divide dividir

Review Key Ideas

Have students complete the activity below to make sure that they understand the lesson concept.

Con tu compañero(a) muestra dos diferentes maneras que puedes usar para dividir $27,542 entre 11 personas.	With a partner show two different methods you can use to divide $27,542 among 11 people.

Applying Mathematics

Preview Key Ideas

Briefly preview key ideas of the lesson in the students' primary language so that students can better comprehend the English instruction.

Hoy practicamos las destrezas de la división que hemos aprendido en este capítulo.	Today we will practice division skills that we have learned throughout the chapter.

Access Vocabulary

Before or during the lesson, be sure to clarify the terms below:

silly (*Teacher's Edition Vol 2* p. 536B) nonsense, foolish, does not make sense
costume (*Student Edition* p. 537) an outfit worn in order to look like or appear as someone else
minivan (*Student Edition* p. 537) a small family van typically used to transport people
food bank (*Student Edition* p. 537) a place to collect food and then give it to people that need it

Spanish Cognates

These words take advantage of what students and their families may know in their home language in order to accelerate the acquisition of math concepts in English.

quotient cociente
process proceso
unit unidad
acceptable aceptable

Review Key Ideas

Have students complete the activity below to make sure that they understand the lesson concept.

Con tu compañero(a) haz un ejemplo visual de tales problemas imposibles para reforzar el concepto de que las matemáticas necesitan tener sentido. Por ejemplo, 4 gatos están sentados encima del basurero. Una pelota le pega a unos de los gatos. ¿Cuántos gatos se quedan? Ninguno por qué los otros se espantaron y se fueron.	Work in pairs to develop visual examples of such impossible problems in order to reinforce that the math needs to make sense. For example, 4 cats are sitting on the school trash dumpster. The kick ball knocks one cat off the edge. How many cats are left? There aren't any cats left because the others would be frightened away by the noise of the ball hitting the dumpster.

Finding Averages

Preview Key Ideas

Briefly preview the key ideas of the lesson in the students' primary language so that students can better comprehend the English instruction.

En esta lección vamos a aprender a encontrar el promedio de un conjunto de números. A veces necesitamos saber el promedio de algo para compararlo. Por ejemplo, los padres quisieran saber la edad promedio en que los niños empiezan a hablar para darse cuenta si su bebé se está desarrollando normalmente, o tal vez quisiéramos saber el número promedio de estudiantes en cada salón de clases para que no tengamos muchos o poquitos estudiantes.

In this lesson we will learn to find the average in a set of numbers. We sometimes need to know the average in order to compare. For example, parents might want to know the average age of children when they begin to speak so they can tell if their baby is developing normally, or we might want to know the average number of students in each class so that we don't have too many or too few in one classroom.

Access Vocabulary

Before or during the lesson, be sure to clarify the terms and phrase below:

above average (*Student Edition* p. 553) more than the average
below average (*Student Edition* p. 553) less than or fewer than the average, or less than typical
stacks (*Student Edition* p. 552) items like textbooks that are placed on top of one another
even things out (*Teacher's Edition Vol 2* p. 552B) distributing items to make all piles even or equal
arithmetic mean (*Student Edition* p. 553) average; EL students may know *mean* as "be defined as" or "not kind."
fair (*Student Edition* p. 552) equal or agreeable to everyone involved

Spanish Cognates

These words take advantage of what students and their families may know in their home language in order to accelerate the acquisition of math concepts in English.

option opción
concept concepto

objects objetos
arithmetic aritmética

Review Key Ideas

Have students complete the activity below to make sure that they understand the lesson concept.

*Piensa en maneras en que la palabra **promedio** es usada en nuestro hablar cotidiano así como, ellos son una **familia** promedio. Discute el significado de la frase "una familia promedio." [Respuestas posibles: Una familia promedio se refiere al estilo de vida de la mayoría de las personas en el área.]*

Think of ways the word *average* is used in everyday speech such as, they are an *average family*. Discuss the meaning of the phrase "an average family." [Possible answers: An average family refers to the lifestyle of most people in the area.]

Mean, Median, Mode, and Range

Preview Key Ideas

Briefly preview the key ideas of the lesson in the students' primary language so that students can better comprehend the English instruction.

En esta lección vas a aprender los términos: **el promedio, la mediana, la moda** *y* **el rango.** *El promedio es el número que se usa para representar un grupo de números. Para hallar un tipo de promedio, sumas los números y divides la suma por el número total de números que se sumaron. El rango es la diferencia entre el mayor y el menor de los valores en una serie de números. La* **mediana** *es el número central (en medio) de un conjunto de números. El número que más se repite en un grupo de números es la* **moda.**	In this lesson we are going to learn the terms *average, median, mode,* and *range.* The *average* is "the number that can represent a group of numbers". To find one type of average, we add up the numbers in the set and divide the sum by the total quantity of numbers added. The *range* is "the difference between the greatest and least number in a series of numbers." The *median* is "the midway number value in a set of numbers" and the *mode* is "the number in the set that repeats the most."

Access Vocabulary

Before or during the lesson, be sure to clarify the terms and phrase below:

keep track of (*Student Edition* p. 556) write down and keep a record of
outliers (*Student Edition* p. 558) numbers that are far from the main grouping of other numbers
noticeably (*Student Edition* p. 558) easily seen as
salaries (*Teacher's Edition Vol 2* p. 559A) plural of salary; fixed sum of money paid to someone at regular intervals for work that is done

Spanish Cognates

These words take advantage of what students and their families may know in their home language in order to accelerate the acquisition of math concepts in English.

range rango
salary salario
to represent representar
situations situaciones
idea idea
group grupo
to invite invitar

IDIOM — The word *salary* originates from the Latin word for salt, *sal. Sal* is also the Spanish word for salt. Ancient Roman soldiers used to be paid with salt which, at the time was expensive and necessary for good health. Someone who was not a good soldier was "not worth his salt" or not worth what he was paid.

Review Key Ideas

Have students complete the activity below to make sure that they understand the lesson concept.

Define la palabra **promedio** *en su uso matemático. Enseña los pasos que hay que seguir para encontrar el promedio de un conjunto de números.*	Write an explanation of the meaning of the word *average.* Show the steps to find the average of a set of numbers.

Using Mathematics

Preview Key Ideas

Briefly preview the key ideas of the lesson in the students' primary language so that students can better comprehend the English instruction.

Hoy vamos a interpretar y computar datos que vienen de situaciones verdaderas. Vamos a ver ejemplos verdaderos de cuando y cómo usamos el promedio, la mediana, la moda y el rango de conjuntos de números.	Today we will compute and interpret data from real-world situations. We will see real examples of when we need to know and how to use mean, median, mode, and range.

Access Vocabulary

Before or during the lesson, be sure to clarify the words and phrases below:

have his rug cleaned (*Student Edition* p. 560) have a professional cleaning person clean the carpeting
Check to see if your answers make sense. (*Student Edition* p. 560) review answers to see if they fit with what you know to be true about a subject
forward/center/guard (*Student Edition* p. 561) positions for players in sports like basketball
rivarly (*Teacher's Edition Vol 2* p. 560B) competition; the strive against another or others in a contest
bowls (*Student Edition* p. 561) takes part in a game where a ball is rolled to knock over pins at the end of a lane
starters (*Student Edition* p. 561) people who begin something; In this example, the starters are the people who will play when the game begins.

Spanish Cognates

These words take advantage of what students and their families may know in their home language in order to accelerate the acquisition of math concepts in English.

to interpret interpretar
data datos
favorite favorito
series series

Review Key Ideas

Have students complete the activity below to make sure that they understand the lesson concept.

Trabaja con tu grupo pequeño de compañeros para decidir cuál es mejor saber si el promedio, la moda, el rango o la mediana.	Work in small groups to decide which is most helpful to know: the mean, median, mode, or range.

Choosing Reasonable Answers

Preview Key Ideas

Briefly preview the key ideas of the lesson in the students' primary language so that students can better comprehend the English instruction.

En esta lección usaremos operaciones inversas de la multiplicación para practicar con problemas narrativos y aproximar respuestas a problemas de la división. Recuerda que la palabra inverso significa "lo opuesto".	In this lesson we will use the inverse operation of multiplication to practice with word problems and approximate answers to division problems. Remember that the word *inverse* means "the opposite."

Access Vocabulary

Before or during the lesson, be sure to clarify the terms below:

wasabi peas (*Teacher's Edition Vol 2* p. 562B) peas covered with a strong smelling and strong tasting Japanese condiment
shortcuts (*Student Edition* p. 562) a way to arrive at an answer or destination by taking fewer steps or a shorter path
estimating (*Teacher's Edition Vol 2* p. 562–563) a judgment or opinion, about the value, quality, size, or cost of something
approximate (*English Learner Support Guide* p. 137) to come near or close to an answer

Spanish Cognates

These words take advantage of what students and their families may know in their home language in order to accelerate the acquisition of math concepts in English.

division división
operation operación
to approximate aproximar
calorie caloría
volunteer voluntario
comics cómicas

Review Key Ideas

Have students complete the activity below to make sure that they understand the lesson concept.

Con tus compañeros describe un ejemplo de cuando sería mejor estimar una respuesta que computar una respuesta exacta. Haz una ilustración del ejemplo.	Work together to describe an example of when it would be better to estimate an answer than to compute an exact answer. Draw an illustration of your example.

Using a Bar Graph

Preview Key Ideas

Briefly preview the key ideas of the lesson in the students' primary language so that students can better comprehend the English instruction.

En esta lección vamos a aprender sobre gráficas de barras. Las gráficas de barras son usadas para mostrar información que se pueda leer de un vistazo. Es común mostrar muchos tipos de datos en una gráfica de barras como las temperaturas diarias, las preferencias de los que responden a una encuesta o para comparar cantidades vendidas de diferentes productos. Las gráficas de barras son buenas para la comparación de datos.	In this lesson we are going to learn about bar graphs. Bar graphs are used to show information that can be read at a quick glance. Many kinds of information are typically shown on a bar graph such as daily temperatures, preferences of people taking a survey, or products sold in stores. Bar graphs are used for comparing data.

Access Vocabulary

Before or during the lesson, be sure to clarify the terms below:

investing (*Student Edition* p. 568) putting money to use for the purpose of obtaining profit or income

car wash (*Student Edition* p. 568) a business where people bring their car to be washed by a machine or by a group of people

bar graph (*Student Edition* p. 568) a visual display of information that shows comparisons at a glance

biggest jump (*Teacher's Edition Vol 2* p. 568B) the largest increase or rise on the chart

misleading (*Teacher's Edition Vol 2* p. 568–569) leading to wrong thought or action

Spanish Cognates

These words take advantage of what students and their families may know in their home language in order to accelerate the acquisition of math concepts in English.

graph gráfica
bar barra
unique único

Review Key Ideas

Have students complete the activity below to make sure that they understand the lesson concept.

Trabaja con un grupo de compañeros para describir un ejemplo de cómo se puede malinterpretar la información en una gráfica. Describe algunas preguntas que deberías hacer cuando miras gráficas para asegurarte que no estas errado.	Work in small groups to give an example of how the information provided on a graph could be misleading. Describe a few questions you should ask when looking at graphs to make sure that you are not being misled.

Interpreting Circle Graphs

Preview Key Ideas

Briefly preview the key ideas of the lesson in the students' primary language so that students can better comprehend the English instruction.

En esta lección nos introducirá un nuevo método de organizar y mostrar datos. Se llama gráfica circular. La comparamos con la gráfica de barras para ver cuando sería más útil usarla.	In this lesson we will add a new method of organizing and displaying data: a circle graph. We will compare it to a bar graph to see when a circle graph is most useful.

Access Vocabulary

Before or during the lesson, be sure to clarify the terms below:

frozen yogurt (*Student Edition* p. 570) a cold, creamy dessert that resembles ice cream but is made from yogurt

main course (*Student Edition* p. 570) During a meal that is served in a series of parts, the *main course* is the most important or largest part.

slices (*Student Edition* p. 570) wedges; triangular-shaped pieces from a pie chart

Spanish Cognates

These words take advantage of what students and their families may know in their home language in order to accelerate the acquisition of math concepts in English.

circle círculo
to report reportar
to represent representar
favorite favorito
to organize organizar

Review Key Ideas

Have students complete the activity below to make sure that they understand the lesson concept.

Trabaja con un grupo pequeño de compañeros para discutir las diferencias que existen entre las gráficas de barras y las gráficas circulares. Incluye ejemplos de alguna información que podrías encontrar en una gráfica circular.	Work in small groups to discuss the differences between bar graphs and circle graphs. Include examples of information you would find on a circle graph.

Tree Diagrams

Preview Key Ideas

Briefly preview the key ideas of the lesson in the students' primary language so that students can better comprehend the English instruction.

Esta lección nos presenta otro organizador de datos. Se llama tree diagram *o diagrama en forma de árbol. Se usa en las situaciones cuando queremos ver todos los diferentes resultados posibles.*	In this lesson we are presented with another data organizer. It is called a *tree diagram*. It is used in situations when we want to see all the different possible outcomes.

Access Vocabulary

Before or during the lesson, be sure to clarify the terms below:

caps (*Student Edition* p. 572) a cloth hat with a visor
outcomes (*Teacher's Edition Vol 2* p. 573) end results or answers
outfits (*Teacher's Edition Vol 2* p. 572–573) pants, shirts, and items such as jewelry or hats that match and are worn together

Spanish Cognates

These words take advantage of what students and their families may know in their home language in order to accelerate the acquisition of math concepts in English.

possible posible
menu menú
buffet bufé

Review Key Ideas

Have students complete the activity below to make sure that they understand the lesson concept.

Escribe en qué se parecen un árbol y un diagrama en forma de árbol (tree diagram).	Write an explanation of how a tree and a tree diagram are similar.

English/Spanish Cognates

These patterns may help students make connections between English and Spanish words.

English words that end with *-tion* are generally the same in Spanish as words that end in *-ción* or *-sión*.

Operation	Operación
Notation	Notación
Addition	Adición
Subtraction	Sustracción
Multiplication	Multiplicación
Division	División
Rotation	Rotación
Fraction	Fracción
Equation	Ecuación
Function	Función

English words that end with *-or* are almost always the same in Spanish.

Factor	Factor
Numerator	Numerador
Denominator	Denominador
Error	Error
Color	Color
Divisor	Divisor

English words that end with *-al* are almost always the same in Spanish.

Final	Final
Equal	Igual
Decimal	Decimal
Differential	Diferencial
Vertical	Vertical
Horizontal	Horizontal
Ordinal	Ordinal
Total	Total

English words that end with *-ive* often are the same as Spanish words ending with *-ivo*.

Positive	Positivo
Negative	Negativo
Expensive	Expensivo
Perspective	Perspectivo
Relative	Relativo

English words that end with *-meter* are the same as Spanish words ending with *-metro*.

Millimeter	Milímetro
Centimeter	Centímetro
Decimeter	Decímetro
Meter	Metro
Decameter	Decámetro
Hectometer	Hectómetro
Kilometer	Kilómetro

Spanish Cognates

These words are the same or nearly the same in English and in Spanish.

A

addition = adición

algorithm = algoritmo

angles = ángulos

area = área

B

bills = billetes

C

calendar = calendario

census = censo

cent = centavo

centimeters = centímetros

chart = gráfico

(to) classify = clasificar

color = color

(to) combine = combinar

common = común

(to) compare = comparar

(to) complete = completar

cone = cono

congruent = congruente

coordinates = coordenadas

(to) copy = copiar

correct = correcto

(to) count = contar

cube = cubo

cylinder = cilindro

D

(to) determine = determinar

diagonal = diagonal

diagrams = diagramas

differences = diferencias

different = diferente

distance = distancia

(to) divide = dividir

dollar = dólar

double = doble

E

equal = igual

equilateral = equilátero

F

false = falso

figure = figura

fraction = fracción

function = función

G

grams = gramos

graph = gráfica

group = grupo

H

horizontal = horizontal

hours = horas

I

inequality signs = signos de desigualdad

intersection = intersección

inverse = inverso

isosceles = isósceles

K

kilometer = kilómetro

L

lesson = lección

line = línea

liters = litros

M

map = mapa

minus = menos

minutes = minutos

N

number = número

P

pattern = patrón

percent = por ciento

perimeter = perímetro

population = población

(to) practice = practicar

proportion = proporción

Q

quadrilateral = cuadrilátero

quart = cuarto

R

rectangle = rectángulo

relation = relación

S

scale = escala

segments = segmentos

signs = signos

strategy = estrategia

sums = sumas

symmetry = simetría

T

table = tabla

temperature = temperatura

thermometer = termómetro

triangle = triángulo

two-digit = dos-dígitos

V

version = versión

vertical = vertical

Z

zero = cero